HOW TO
MAKE
MONEY
TRADING
LISTED PUTS

HOW TO
MAKE
MONEY
TRADING
LISTED PUTS

By
Lin Tso

Cover Design by Gloria Tso

Fell's Books Fill Your Needs

FREDERICK FELL PUBLISHERS, INC., NEW YORK

Library of Congress Cataloging in Publication Data

Tso, Lin, security analyst.
    How to make money trading listed puts.

    Includes index.
    1. Put and call transactions.   I.   Title.
HG6041.T77   332.6'45   78-9295
ISBN 0-8119-0295-1

For information address:

Frederick Fell Publishers, Inc.
386 Park Avenue South
New York, New York 10016

Published simultaneously in Canada by:
Thomas Nelson & Sons, Limited
Don Mills, Ontario, Canada

MANUFACTURED IN THE UNITED STATES OF AMERICA

1 2 3 4 5 6 7 8 9 0

Designed by Michael U. Polvere

DEDICATION

Once Again, As Always,

To My Dearest Sou Cheng

For Her Love, Devotion, and Unbounded Help

Contents

INTRODUCTION ....

Part I
FUNDAMENTALS AND TECHNIQUES

1 PUT BASICS 3
  Analysis Of Basic Components 3
    A Call In Reverse 3
    Put Option Components 4

  Mental Gear Shifting 6
    Radically Different 6
    Reverse Concept Of In-And-Out-Of-The-Money 6
    In-The-Money Puts 6
    Out-Of-The-Money Puts 7
    Cost And Leverage Comparisons 8

  Two Sides To The Game 8
    Buying Side 8
    Selling Side 9

  How To Calculate Put Premiums 9
    Put Premiums 9
    Inverse Relationship to Stock Price 10

  Major Factors Determining Put Premiums 10
    The Underlying Stock Price Relative To The Strike Price ..11
    The Length Of Time Remaining Until Expiration 11
    The Volatility Of The Underlying Stock 11

2 FOCUSING ON SIMPLE STRATEGIES 13
  From The Put Buyer's Viewpoint 14
    First Simple Strategy—Buying A Put 14
    Second Simple Strategy—Buying Stock, Buying A Put 15

From the Put Seller's Viewpoint 16
Third Simple Strategy—Selling A Put 16
Fourth Simple Strategy—Selling Stock Short,
Selling A Put 17

Summary Of Simple Strategies 18
Simple Buying Strategies 18
Simple Selling Strategies...........................19

Part II
PUT BUYING

3 PUT BUYING: WHY AND HOW 23
Three Important Reasons For Buying..................23
Risk Limitation 24
Similar Vs. Dissimilar Aspects 24
Covered Vs. Uncovered Put Buying 25
Principal Uses 25

4 LONG PUT 28
Three Main Applications 28
Speculation 28
Short-Sale Alternative 30
Leverage 30
Limited Risk 34
No Margin Call 34
Salvage Value 34
Flexibility In Timing 34
Instead Of Stop-Loss Order 35
No Cash Dividend Liability 35
Protection 35
Shielding Profit....................................35
How The Protection Works 36
The Lesser Evil 36
Why Particularly For Volatile Stocks 37

When And What Puts To Buy 37
Choose Which Put To Buy 37
Absolute Vs. Relative Risks 38
Above Or Below Strike Price At Expiration.............38

To Sell Or To Exercise 39
  Two Alternate Courses 39
  Third Approach....................................41

Put Buying As A Trading Vehicle 41
  Locking In A Short-Sale Profit 41
  Averaging Down On A Short Position 42
  Trading For Down Fluctuations.....................42
  Using Puts To Diversify 42

Alternative Risk-Minimizing Vehicle 42
  Two Choices 42
  Disadvantages 43
  Advantages 44
  Sell-Stop 44

5 LONG PUT, LONG STOCK 45
  Buy Put, Buy Stock 45
  Protective Premium................................45
  Complete Vs. Partial Hedge 46
  Two Major Categories 46

Protecting Existing Positions 47
  Safeguarding Unrealized Profits 47

Protecting New Purchases 49
  Establishing Minimum Liquidating Price 49
  "Married Put" 50

Long Put, Long Stock vs. Long Put,
Long Call...51
  Long Put Plus Long Stock 51
  Long Put Plus Long Call............................51

Part III
PUT SELLING

6 PUT SELLING: WHY AND HOW 55
  Potential Risk and Reward 55
  Put Writer (Seller) 55

Analysis Of Obligations 56
   Meaning Of Exercise Notice 56
   Closing Of A Purchase Transaction 56

Covered Vs. Uncovered Put Writing 57
   "Short Put" Vs. "Short Pub, Short Stock" 57
   Analysis Of Naked Put Selling 57
   Risk Vs. Reward Potential.............................59
   Differences 60

How To Choose Which Put To Write 61
   Choice Of Exercise Price 61

Put Writing Margins 63
   Different Margin Concept.............................63
   Margin Exceptions 63

7 SHORT PUT 64
   Writing Against Cash.................................64
   Known Vs. Unknown Risk 64
   Be Financially Prepared 65
   Expecting A Rising Or Stable Stock 65

Step-By-Step Writing Procedure.........................65
   Initial Put-Writing Position...........................66
   Initial Margin Requirement 66
   Maintenance Margin Requirement 66
   Potential Results At Different Stock Price Levels 66
   Option Profit Levels 67
   When And How To Close Out 68
   Not That Naked 68

To Earn Premium Income 69
   Adding To Dividends.................................69
   Two Ways of Earning Premium Income 69

To Acquire Stock At Below Market Price 71
   Why Not Pay Less? 71
   Establishing An Effective Cost 71
   Key Consideration 71

Another Method Of Lowering Purchase Price 72
Investment Flexibility 73
In-The-Money Vs. Out-of-The-Money Put Writing 74

Multiple-Exercise-Price Put Writing 75
Different Exercise Prices 75

How To Measure Volatility 77
Meaning Of Beta 77
Which Direction? To What Extent? 77
Key Consideration 78

Means Of Defense 78
Concept Of Defense 78
Basic Ground Rules 78
Defense Strategies Against Adverse Stock Action 79
Defense #1: Naked Call Writing .79
Defense #2: Selling Stock Short .79
Defense #3: Selling Stock Short Plus Call Writing 79

8 SHORT PUT, SHORT STOCK 80
Hedged Put Writing 80
Only Partially covered 80
High-Risk Bear Strategy 81

How To Select The Strike Price 83
Considerable Flexibility 83

9 SHORT PUT, LONG STOCK 86
Writing Either With Or Without Stock Ownership 86
Double Leverage 87

Part IV
PUT SPREADING

10 PUT SPREADING—WHY AND HOW 91
Why & How 91
Basic Concept 91
Dollar Difference 92
"Relative" Vs. "Absolute" 92

"Simultaneous" Long And Short 93
Meaning of "Debit" vs. "Credit" 93

Spread Construction 94
Varying Spread Combinations 94
Principal Spread Forms.................................94
Value Deviation 95
Potential Risk And Reward 96
Commission And Tax Factors 96

Put Spread Margins 97
General Put Margin Requirements 97
Put Margin Calculations 97

11 PUT TIME SPREADS 100
Principle Of Put Time Spreading 100
Different Expiration Months 100
How To Widen Spread 101
Two Key Factors 102
Two Ways To Profitability............................103
Key To Sound Spreading 103

Three Principal Approaches 104
Bullish, Bearish Or Neutral 104
Neutral Approach—Using At-The-Money Puts 104
Bullish Approach—Using In-The-Money Puts...........105
Rolling A Bullish Put Time Spread 106
Bearish Approach—Using Out-Of-The-Money Puts 107
Bearish Put Time Spread Vs. Bearish Call Time Spread ..108

12 PUT PRICE SPREADS 109
Vertical Structure 109

Bullish Approach—Sell Higher
Strike, Buy Lower Strike 110
Risk In One-Sided Simple Buying....................110
Risk-Reducing Element 110

How To Calculate Potential Spread Profit/Risk 112
Calculation Of Potential Spread Profit 112
Calculation Of Potential Spread Risk 112

How To Maximize Spread Profit/Risk 113
Calculation Of Spread Break-even Point 113
5-Point vs. 10-Point Spread Calculations 113

Bearish Approach—Buy Higher Strike, Sell Lower Strike ...115
Instead Of Simple-Buying Strategy 115
Risk/Reward Potential 115
How To Widen A Bear Put Price Spread 116

How To Roll A Bear Put Price Spread 117
Original Put Price Spread Structure 117
New Bear Put Price Structure 117

Part V
OTHER MULTIPLE OPTIONS

13 STRADDLES 121
Straddle: Why and How 121
Most Common Combination.....................121
Need Not Know Market Direction 122
How To Calculate Upper And Lower Profit Levels 122
General Ground Rules.............................123

Long Straddle 124
Importance of Volatility 124
Other Key Criteria...................................124
Which Expiration Month to Choose 124
Basic Straddle Analysis 124

Short Straddle 126
Selling Put And Call On Same Stock, Same Strike,
Same Expiration 126
Risk of "Whipsaw" 128

Bullish Vs. Bearish Approach 128
Bullish Approach—Using Out-Of-The-Money Puts 128
Bearish Approach—Using In-The-Money Puts 129

Short Straddle, Long Stock 131
With Or Without Related Stock Position 131

Short Straddle Alone 131
Combining Short Straddle With Long Stock 133
How To Reduce Risk In A Short Straddle 134

How To Calculate Straddle Margins 135
Margin On A Long Straddle........................135
Margin On A Short Straddle 136

14 COMBINATIONS...........................137
Objectives Of Combinations 137
Importance of Volatility..............................137
Broad Vs. Narrow Meaning 138

Combination Buying 139
Combination On The Same Expiration Month 139
Long Call, Long Put (With Different Strike Prices) 139
Method Of Calculation 140
Step-By-Step Procedure 141
Two Basic Approaches..............................142
Bullish Vs. Bearish Approach 143
With Or Without Underlying Stock Position 145
Variable Ratio Combination Buying 146

Combination Selling................................148
Short Call, Short Put (With Different Strike Prices) 148
Seeking A Static Stock..............................148
With Or Without Related Stock Position 148
Uncovered Combination Seller 148
Covered Combination Seller 152
Combination Seller With Short Stock Position 152
Varied Ratio Approach..............................152
Evaluating Each Component 153

Combination Vs. Straddle 153
Relative Dollar Risks 153
Combination Buying Vs. Straddle Buying 154
Combination Sale Vs. Straddle Sale 154

15 PUT MARGINS 155
Minimum Margin Requirements 156

Long Put 156

Long Put, Long Stock 157
   Initial Margin Requirement 157
   Maintenance Margin Requirement 157

Short Put 157
   In-The-Money 158
   Out-Of-The-Money 158

Short Put, Short Stock 159
   Initial Margin Requirement 159
   Maintenance Margin Requirement 159

Put Spread Margins 160
   General Spread Margin Rules 160
   Margins For Put Spreads 160

Straddle Margins 162
   Long Call, Long Put 162
   Short Call, Short Put 163

Combination Margins 164
   Short Call, Short Put With Different Exercise Prices 164

Glossary of Option Terms 166
Put Options Questionnaire 175

INTRODUCTION

Making Money In Down Markets

With the advent of listed puts, the age-old battle of wits for profit for stock traders and investors promises to never be quite the same again.

For most speculative traders, speculating on stock price changes has traditionally meant speculating on stock price *increases*. But as stock market gyrations of recent years have clearly shown, price changes are by no means always price increases. Stock prices *can*—and normally *do—drop*, as quickly and as precipitously as they can rise.

Traditionally, traders and speculators rely primarily on selling (stock) short as a means of making money in stocks they believe are likely to go down. In a short sale, a person sells borrowed stock in the hope of buying it back later—a process known as "covering"—at a lower price, and thus realizing a profit on the difference between the sale and purchase prices.

Conceptually, the idea of selling something they don't own is hard for many investors to grasp. Moreover, short selling exposes traders and speculators to unlimited risks, if the stock should go up instead of going down, because short sellers would have to "cover" or buy back borrowed stock at higher prices. Also, they would expose themselves to the possibility of margin calls.

A New, Practical Investment Tool

Thus, up until now most investors haven't had a practical investment vehicle with which to speculate on the down side of stock price movements. Puts can provide such a vehicle. A put is an option which gives the buyer the right to *sell* 100 shares of stock at a fixed price during a fixed period of time, whereas the more familiar call is an option which gives the buyer the right to *buy* similar securities.

An investor who has grown accustomed to the "up together, down together" relationship between stock and call option prices must learn to mentally "shift gears" when thinking of put options. As stock prices decline, prices of call options go down, whereas those of put options do the reverse and increase in value.

Essentially, puts offer a cheap way—and a highly-leveraged and limited-risk way of shorting the market, but that's a tough concept for the average investor, who typically thinks in terms of bigger and better as the American way.

What makes put buying a cheap way of shorting stocks? Consider this example provided by the Chicago Board Options Exchange:

Assume that on July 1 the common stock of Manufacturing Company (M.F.G.) is selling at $50 a share. An investor expecting a decline in the stock price decides to purchase an M.F.G./JAN 50 put option for $5 a share. That's $500 for a 100-share put.

Now assume that by Nov. 1 the price of the stock has declined to $42 a share. The right to sell the stock at $50 has become more valuable, and the put is bid to $9 a share. The 100-share put bought at $500 can thus be sold for $900—resulting in a $400 gain, less commissions.

The $400 gain on a $500 investment represents an 80 percent rate of return (less commissions, of course), and it illustrates the leverage a trader can achieve by purchasing puts.

In the above example, JAN refers to January, when the option expires, and 50 is the strike price. The two types of options—calls and puts—have similar terms (expiration month, strike price, etc.) except that the *call* is an option to *buy*, while the *put* is an option to sell.

Let's further assume that the same person had decided instead to sell short 100 shares of M.F.G. at $50 a share. This would require a margin deposit of 50 percent, or $2,500. Thus, the $800 gain realized when the short sale was covered at $42 would have represented only a 32 percent return on investment.

Also, consider the factor of limited risk. No matter how sharply the price of M.F.G. might rise, the buyer cannot lose more than the $500 he paid for the put—in contrast to the unlimited risk inherent in selling short.

High-Leverage But Limited Risk

Thus, in contrast to short sale of stock—a method many investors shun because of the complexities and substantial upside price risk—the purchase of listed puts offers a number of advantages: known and predetermined risks, greater leverage, and freedom from the expense and annoyance of margin calls, among other things.

Buying puts as an alternative to short sale is but one of many uses for this new exciting investment tool. Just as in the case of call options, put options offer opportunities for profit and opportunities for protection. In particular, however, listed put options offer an investment vehicle that may be especially attractive to the individual who seeks a way to participate in the securities market during periods of declining stock prices.

The availability of listed puts give investors a better balanced market perspective—a perspective in which the search for profit opportunities is no longer necessarily linked to rising stock prices. Put options make it as easy to invest for profit in "down" markets as in "up" markets. This is because, all else being equal, a decrease in the value of the stock generally results in an increase in the value of a put.

Put options are, of course, not free of risk. They're not for widows and orphans, or probably not for those investors who can't afford to lose the price paid for the option. The put buyer will lose his entire stake, if a put expires worthless. For those investors, however, who understand how puts work and how they can be used, the ability to participate in declining markets as well as rising markets can mean a greatly expanded number of money-making opportunities. Options are not inherently speculative. It is the ways in which options are used which tend to be either speculative or conservative. Just as in the case of call options, there are situations in which put options can be used to advantage in both types of strategies.

From The Simple To The Complex
This book is designed to provide investors with fundamental information concerning the possible uses, risks and rewards of listed put option trading. While the availability of listed puts has opened up virtually unlimited combinations of investment and trading strategies, we start with an explanation of the basics and then proceed from the simple to the more complex topics.

Throughout the book we stress the importance of step-by-step learning by using simple and easy-to-understand illustrations based on actual stock and option prices. For the sake of simplicity, such illustrations exclude commissions and tax considerations that are important in actual transactions.

I wish to express my heartfelt thanks to Mr. Edwin Burton, director of options at Smith Barney, Harris, Upham & Co. who took the trouble of reading the entire manuscript and offered many valuable suggestions.

LIN TSO
New York City

Part I

FUNDAMENTALS AND TECHNIQUES

Chapter 1

PUT BASICS

What:
A put option is a mirror image of a call option. Whereas a call is an option to *buy* stock at a specific price, a put is an option to *sell* stock at a specific price.

Why:
Puts are primarily bear market instruments, permitting the average investor to participate in an anticipated stock price decline without the risk of a short seller.

How:
A put option becomes more valuable as the market price of the stock declines. The put gives the holder the right to sell stock at a predetermined (exercise) price regardless of how sharply the stock price may decline. In return for selling this right, the put writer (seller) receives a premium.

ANALYSIS OF BASIC COMPONENTS

A Call In Reverse
What is a listed put option? To begin with, a put option is a call option in reverse. Its nomenclature, strike price, premium, expiration month, etc. is exactly the same. The difference is that whereas a call is an option to *buy* shares of stock at a specific price (the strike price), a put is an option to *sell* shares of stock at the specified strike price.

As the mirror image of a call option, the put option gives its owner the right to sell 100 shares of an underlying stock at a specified price known as the strike or exercise price, any time before the option expires. In contrast, a call option gives the holder the right to buy underlying stock under similar conditions.

At the expense of some repetition for readers already familiar with the basics through their knowledge of call options, we will start with a brief description of the terms used in daily option quotations such as the one below that appears in the Wall Street Journal and in the financial pages of many daily newspapers.

Illustration

At the close of October 14, 1977 Eastman Kodak had the following price data:

Underlying Security	Strike Price	Expiration Month			Close
		Oct.	Jan.	Apr.	
Eas. Kd.	60	$3/16$	2¼	3⅝	58⅛
Eas Kd P	60	2⅛	3⅝	4⅝	58⅛

The letter "P" following the underlying security's name and strike price denotes a put. Quotations without the "P" are calls.

Put Option Components

The above data provides a convenient way to introduce the components of a put option:

1. *The Underlying Security*

    This is the common stock on which the option is traded. "Eas Kd" is the abbreviation for Eastman Kodak.
    • An Eas Kd put option is the option to *sell* 100 shares of Eas Kd common stock. (The Eas Kd call option is the option to *buy* 100 shares of stock).

2. *The Strike Price*

    This is the price per share at which the buyer of the put option may—during the life of the option—exercise his right to *sell* the shares of stock to a writer of a put option.

    The strike price in the above illustration is $60 per share.

4

(Similarly, the Eas Kd call option is the right to *buy* 100 shares of the stock at $60 per share).

3. *The Expiration Month*

This is the month in which the option expires (on the Saturday following the third Friday).

All listed options expire quarterly—some on a January/April/July/October quarterly cycle and others on quarterly cycles beginning in either February or March. At any given time, options are traded in the cycle's nearest three expiration months.

In the above illustration, for instance, Eas Kd put and call options were presently being traded with expirations in October, January and April.

4. *The Premium*

This is the sum of money (dollars per share) a put option buyer would have paid—and a put option writer would have received—if the purchase and sale were at the same prices as the closing prices for this particular day.

Note that for an Eas Kd Jan. 60 put option the buyer would have paid $362.50 (3⅝ per share) and the seller would have received $362.50.

The option premium is kept by the writer of the option regardless of whether it is exercised or not. (In the same quotation, the price of an Eas Kd Jan 60 call option was $225 (2¼ per share).

5. *The Close*

This is the closing price of the underlying stock.

Since put option trading has always been considered a part of the natural evolvement of listed options, most call rules were originally written with puts in mind. A conscious effort has been made to avoid radical put-call variations within the rules.

The contract terms for listed puts are based on the same standardized procedures used for listed calls. Puts trade with the same expiration cycles as calls, with similarly determined strike prices, dilution protection and the like.

5

MENTAL GEAR SHIFTING

While puts and calls are similar in form, they differ in substance.

Radically Different

In many respects puts are radically different from calls. Firstly, the meanings of in-the-money and out-of-the-money are diametrically different for puts as opposed to calls.

At this point we need a mental gear shifting to understand in-the-money and out-of-the-money puts, which are precisely the opposite of in-the-money and out-of-the-money calls.

Reverse Concept Of In- and Out-Of-The-Money

The following illustrates the reverse concepts of in-the-money and out-of-the-money calls versus in-the-money and out-of-the-money puts.

1. Calls Stock Price	Call Strike Price
$40	$35 (in-the-money)
$40	$40 (on-the-money)
$40	$45 (out-of-the-money)

2. Puts Stock Price	Put Strike Price
$40	$35 (out-of-the-money)
$40	$40 (on-the-money)
$40	$45 (in-the-money)

In-the-Money Puts

At expiration of the option, a put is "in the money" if its strike price is *above* the market price of the underlying stock. The put's value should approximate the difference between the strike price and the market price.

The value of a put at expiration therefore hinges on *how much*, if at all, the option allows you to sell the stock at above its current market price.

Illustration

At Oct. 14, 1977 closing, Eastman Kodak (Eas Kd) had the following price data on its April 70 put:

Stock	Strike price	Apr. Put Price	Stock Price
EAS KD	70	12½	58⅛

Based on the above price data, an Eas Kd April put that conveys the *right* to *sell* 100 shares of Eas Kd stock at $70 per share has the following value components:

Intrinsic value 11⅞ (70-58⅛)
Time value ....⅝ (12½-11⅞)

Total value 12½

As expiration nears, the time value will disappear and the price of the in-the-money put will be approximately the intrinsic value of 11⅞ ($1,187.50 for the 100-share option).

In this and other examples in this book, for the sake of simplicity we exclude both commission costs and taxes that can be significant.

Out-Of-The-Money Puts

If the stock price at expiration is *above* the strike price, the put is "out-of-the-money" and should expire worthless.

Illustration

At its Oct. 14, 1977 closing, Santa Fe International (SAF) and its underlying stock had the following price relationship:

Stock	Strike Price	October Put Price	Stock Price
SAF Put	45	3/16	46½

The SAF Oct 45 put had no intrinsic value as the stock price was *above* the strike price. The 3/16 price tag for the put option was for the remaining time value of 5 days before it expires Oct. 19, 1977.

7

To summarize, a put is out-of-the-money when the underlying stock price is *above* the strike price and is in-the-money when the underlying stock price is *below* the strike price. A call is just the reverse, that is, it is out-of-the-money when the underlying stock is *below* the strike price and is in-the-money when the stock price is *above* the strike price.

Cost And Leverage Comparisons

Since an in-the-money put already has some intrinsic value, it generally costs more. It will move more closely with the stock in declining markets. On the other hand, an investor would lose his entire put premium on an advance in the stock.

On the other hand, since an out-of-the-money put has no intrinsic value, it will cost less. In the event of a substantial decline in the stock price, an out-of-the-money put provides greater leverage because of its smaller dollar investment and, of course, with less dollars at risk. However, relative to the in-the-money put, the underlying stock will have to decline a greater percentage before an out-of-the-money put begins to gain intrinsic value.

TWO SIDES TO THE GAME

Just as call options have two sides to the game, put options also involve buying on the one side and selling on the other.

Buying Side

On the buying side, a trader buys a call option when he believes the underlying stock will rise in value, and buys a put option when he thinks the underlying stock will decline in value.

Calls are essentially bull market instruments, permitting investors to participate in the anticipated rise in the price of the underlying stock at a fraction of the cost required for outright stock ownership.

On the other hand, puts are primarily bear market instruments, permitting the average investor to participate without the undue risk of the short sale of the underlying stock. To go short would require capital the average investor normally does not have.

Keep in mind that a buyer of a call is similar to an owner of

8

100 shares of stock, with no more risk than the cost of the call, and that a buyer of a put is similar to a short-seller, with his entire risk confined to the cost of the put.

The most you can lose when you buy a put option is its total cost. But such a total loss will normally occur only if you continue to hold the option and it expires worthless. If the option is sold prior to its expiration, you should recover part of the premium because of its remaining time value.

Illustration

Assume that on July 27, 1977, you paid 2¼ for a Dec 40 put on Revlon (RLM) while the stock was 39¾.

The stock rose to 43¼ as of Sept 14, 1977 while its Dec 40 put declined to ⅞. If you liquidated the put for ⅞ at this point (with three more months remaining until expiration), your loss would be 1⅜ (2¼-⅞) before commissions, instead of a total loss.

Selling Side

On the selling side, an investor sells (writes) a call option when he thinks the stock will either flat or fall, and sells (writes) a put option when he believes the underlying stock will go up.

From a writer's point of view, puts will make option writing a year-round activity, since writers who don't want to sell calls in an up market can then write puts.

HOW TO CALCULATE PUT PREMIUMS

Put Premiums

At this point you might well wonder how the price of puts or put option premiums are arrived at—and what factors cause them to increase or decrease. Generally, the supply and demand factor for puts has determined put premium levels.

In the over-the-counter market, puts generally are at a substantial discount to calls. This is so because of greater demand for calls and straddles than for puts.

A straddle is a combination option, consisting of a call option and a put option, with the same strike price and the same expiration on the same underlying stock. Conversion houses create calls by breaking straddles apart and pricing puts lower to cover certain costs.

In the listed options market, if a put and a call have the same terms (same underlying stock, expiration date and strike price), and if the stock is selling at the strike price, the put generally remains priced somewhat lower than the call. One reason for this is that the stock can theoretically move farther to the upside than to the downside, because stock can only decrease by 100%, but can increase by much more than that.

Put option premiums, like call option premiums, are influenced by changes in the price of the underlying stock. But the price relationships are just the opposite.

Inverse Relationship To Stock Price

All else remaining the same, as the price of the *stock decreases*, the *put premium* tends to *increase*. This is because the right which the put conveys—the *right* to *sell* shares of the stock at a specific price—becomes more valuable as the market price of the stock declines.

Illustration

Assume you buy a put option with a strike price of $60. This gives you a locked-in-right—at any time during the life of the option—to sell the stock at that price, regardless of how sharply the market price of the stock declines in the meantime.

Thus, if the market price of the stock drops to $52, the right to sell at $60 could be worth approximately $8 (60-52). Should the stock drop to $50, the right to sell it at $60 could be worth approximately $10 (60-50). And so on, with the increased value being reflected in an increased option premium.

Exactly the opposite is true of call options. All else remaining the same, as the price of the stock *decreases*, the *call* premium tends to decrease. This is because the right which the call conveys—the *right* to *buy* shares of the stock at a specific price—becomes less valuable as the market price of the stock declines.

MAJOR FACTORS DETERMINING PUT PREMIUMS

The three major factors determining put option premiums are (1) the current market price of the underlying stock relative to the strike price of the option, (2) the length of time remaining until expiration of the option and (3) the volatility of the underlying stock.

1. The underlying stock price relative to the strike price

Since the put strike price is a fixed dollar amount, it follows that (all else remaining the same) decreases in the market price of the underlying stock will tend to result in an increase in the put premium. On the other hand, an increase in the price of the underlying stock will tend to reduce the put premium.

At expiration, the put option premium should be approximately the amount, if any, that the option strike price is above the then current market value of the underlying stock. If the strike price happens to be below the market price of the stock, the option should expire worthless.

Illustration

On Sept. 13, 1977, Hughes Tool (HT) closed at 35⅞ while its Sept. 40 put was at 4½. Since the September option would expire four days later (on the 17th), the put price at 4½ reflected mostly its intrinsic value of 4⅛ (40-35⅞). The balance,. ⅜ (4½-4⅛), represented the remaining 4-day time value.

Had the market price of HT been above the put strike price of 40, the put option at expiration would have been worthless.

2. The length of time remaining until expiration

A put, like a call, is a wasting asset; its value decreases as its expiration date approaches. An option that is not worthwhile to exercise at expiration becomes worthless.

3. The volatility of the underlying stock

A major factor in the determination of put values is the volatility of the underlying stock. If large swings in the stock's price are common, option buyers will be willing to pay a larger premium for it, because chances of profit from a large upswing are better. Likewise, the option writer will insist on a larger premium because chances of substantial loss are increased.

11

Investors should know and understand the Beta of the stock underlying the option. The Beta of a stock is the propensity of the stock to move with the market—its price movement volatility. While we believe it is impossible for anyone to accurately predict the price movement of the stock, it is very possible to state whether a particular stock is likely to have a large price movement based upon its historical performance.

The behavior of the stock price movement in the past is invaluable. And the stock with the greatest movement has the highest Beta. It is no coincidence that the options on stocks with the highest Betas are the ones that command the highest premiums, and that stocks with low Betas have low premiums. Higher premiums for higher Beta stocks are based on the greater probability that they are going to move faster and farther than low Beta stocks.

Beside the above three major factors, another key factor determining option premium levels generally are market interest rates.

There are major differences between put pricing and call pricing due to dividend considerations and truncated (0 to 00) price domains.

Chapter 2

FOCUSING ON SIMPLE STRATEGIES

What:
Two simple strategies each for the put buyer and for the put seller:

(1) For the buyer: (a) Long put
                       (b) Long put, Long stock
(2) For the seller: (a) Short put
                       (b) Short put, Short stock

Why:
Put buying offers a desirable alternative to selling stock short because of its two advantages: (1) leverage, and (2) limited risk. It is also used as "insurance" to protect a stock position.

Put selling is primarily for (1) generating cash flow and (2) acquiring stock at below market price.

How:
At the relatively small cost of a put, the put buyer would achieve the same gain as a short seller without the latter's unlimited risk. The put seller expects to pocket the premium money if and when the stock rises, as anticipated, which will render the put written (sold) worthless.

Four Basic Strategies
With the advent of listed puts, possible option strategies increase manyfold through combinations of puts with puts, calls with calls, and calls with puts.

As a way of easing our mental shift into a major new investment tool, we will focus on the simpler put strategies. Essentially, there are four of them, including two each from the put buyer's and the put seller's viewpoint.

From the put buyer's viewpoint, there are
    (1) buying a put, and
    (2) buying stock, buying a put.
From the put seller's viewpoint, there are
    (3) Selling a put and
    (4) Selling stock short, selling a put.

FROM THE PUT BUYER'S VIEWPOINT

First Simple Strategy—Buying A Put

The first simple put strategy is buying puts.

When an investor anticipates a stock rising, his simplest choices are between stock purchase or call purchase. The call purchase has two advantages: Leverage (the possibility of higher percentage returns) and limited downside risk.

Conversely, when an investor expects a stock to go down, his choices are between shorting the stock or buying a put. The put purchase also offers two advantages: leverage (because of the much smaller initial investment) and limited upside risk (versus theoretically no limit on the upside exposure for short sellers). As with a call, the risk to the put holder is limited to 100 percent of his initial investment or the premium paid for the put.

Illustration

On Sept. 9, 1977 Honeywell (HON) had the following puts with the strike prices of 40 and 45:

Strike	Nov	Feb	May	Stock price
45	¾	$1^9/_{16}$	2	47⅝
40	3⅛	3⅞	4⅜	47⅝

If you were only moderately bearish on HON at 47⅝, you could buy a put with a strike price of 45 at ¾ for the November option, or at $1^9/_{16}$ for the February option, or at 2 for the May option, depending upon the time frame within which you believe the stock decline would take place.

If you were extremely bearish on HON at 47⅝, you could buy the more expensive strike price at $40 puts for 3⅛ (November) or for 3⅞ (February) or for 4⅜ (May), again depending on the length of the time period you believe required to have the anticipated price decline in the underlying stock take place.

14

If the stock rises above the strike price, the holder would incur a loss which would be limited to the money you put up for buying the option. Most of the time, however, you wouldn't have to suffer a total loss because you might be able to reduce the loss by selling the put in the secondary market prior to expiration.

If the stock declines, the put holder may realize a profit by either (a) selling the put in the secondary market, or (b) exercising the put by buying stock at the current market price and delivering it against payment of the strike price. In making a choice between the two alternate courses of action you shall be guided by such factors as the current premium for the put in the secondary market, applicable commissions, margin requirements and tax considerations.

Second Simple Strategy—Buying Stock, Buying A Put

The second simple strategy is to combine buying stock with buying a put.

If an investor purchases stock but desires to protect his position against a substantial decline in its market value, he can buy the stock and simultaneously buy a put. Thus, the investor has complete protection against loss no matter how much the stock might decline, since he can always sell the stock at the strike price (assuming that the strike price is the same as the purchase price of the stock). Just as a call option can guarantee the purchase price of a short position, a put option can guarantee the sale price of a long position.

For this downside protection, the investor pays a price for the put as an "insurance" or "offset" against possible correction in the market value of the underlying stock.

Illustrations

At Oct. 20, 1977 closing, you could combine long stock—long put positions on the following four issues and puts:

Stock	Price	Put	Price
AMERADA HESS (AHC)	30	Feb 30	1¾
INEXCO (INX)	20⅛	Feb 20	1½
MESA (MSA)	39⅛	Jan 40	2⅜
NORTHWEST INDUSTRIES(NWT)	51	Dec 50	1⁹/₁₆

15

The cost of combining a long stock position and a long put to protect that long stock position is summarized as follows:

Stock	Cost of Stock	Cost of Put	Total Cost
AHC	30	1¾	31¾
INX	20⅛	1½	21⅝
NWT	51	$1^9/_{16}$	$52^9/_{16}$
MSA	39⅛	2⅜	41½

If the stock price were *above* the strike price of the put option at expiration, the put would be worthless. No one would logically want to exercise a put option to sell stock at the strike price when he can merely go to the open market and sell for a higher price.

On the other hand, if the stock were to decline well *below* the strike price of the put option, the *increase* in the value of the long put position would essentially offset the *decrease* in the value of the long stock position.

In buying a put simultaneously with stock purchase, the investor does not sacrifice the opportunity to participate in increases in the stock price. Any increase in the price of the stock in excess of the price paid for the option (plus transaction costs), will result in a net gain for the investor.

This strategy also applies to helping protect previously acquired stocks. Thus, the holder of a put is able to:

(1) protect long-term capital gains in a stock he wishes to hold indefinitely, and

(2) freeze a capital gain of loss in a stock in a current year and defer the tax consequences to the succeeding year.

FROM THE PUT SELLER'S VIEWPOINT

For every buyer of a put option, there must first be a seller, or writer. The following are two simple put strategies from the seller's point of view.

Third Simple Strategy—Selling A Put

The third simple strategy involving the use of puts is selling (writing) puts.

You sell (write) a put on a stock you believe will rise in value. By writing a put, the seller automatically receives a premium, which varies in amount. In general, the more volatile the underlying stock, the greater the premium. Investors may find writing puts—especially during periods of stable or rising stock prices—can be to their advantage. In simplest terms, put selling offers a method to increase the cash flow for one's investment portfolio.

If, for example, an investor writes a put with a striking price of 60 and receives a premium of $4 a share, that works out to $400 for the 100-share option: if the put is not exercised, the writer is $400 richer. But, of course, it may not work out that way. Selling put options, just like buying puts, involves its own risks and potential rewards.

Let's use an example based on actual prices.

Illustration
At Oct. 24, 1977 closing Inexco (INX) had the following puts available with a strike price at 20:

Strike price	Nov	Feb	May	Stock Price
20	$1^5/_{16}$	2	2⅜	19⅛

If you believed that the recent weakness in INX was likely to be only temporary, you could sell (write) a Nov 20 Put for $1^5/_{16}$, or a Feb 20 Put for 2 or a May 20 Put for 2⅜, depending on your assessment of how long INX would remain weak. If INX should rise in price as anticipated, the put you had sold would become worthless and you would pocket the premium received for selling (writing) the put. Or you could, prior to expiration, realize a gain by closing out your position in the secondary market.

If, on the other hand, the stock price falls below the strike price, you could be assigned an exercise notice. In that event, you would be required to purchase the underlying shares at the strike price, which would be higher than the then current market value. You could immediately liquidate the position and realize a loss or hold the stock for future recovery.

Fourth Simple Strategy—Selling Stock Short, Selling A Put
The fourth simple startegy involving the use of puts is combining short stock sale with selling a put on the stock.

17

Selling stock short is ordinarily considered a speculative investment strategy, but the investor can reduce this risk and earn premium income by hedging through the sale of a put.

If the stock price subsequently declines as expected, the investor can cover his short stock position at a profit and re-purchase his put in the secondary market at a loss. If the profit on the short sale exceeds the loss on the put, he would realize a net gain on the transaction. If, instead, the investor waits to receive an exercise notice, he can use the stock "put" to him to cover his short stock position. In this case, his profit would be the premium originally received upon sale of the put.

If the stock price rose, the investor is still hedged to a certain degree, since the premium income from the put will partially offset his loss from his short position in the stock. Unlike covered call writing, however, risk is unlimited.

Illustration

If, on Oct. 4, 1977, you were bearish on Eastman Kodak (EK) at 60⅜, you could sell EK short at that price and reduce the risk of such a short position by selling an EK Apr 60 Put for 3½.

At Oct. 24, 1977 closing, EK had declined 7¾ points to 52⅝ while EK Apr 60 Put had risen 4⅝ points to 8⅛. You could cover your short stock position at a 7¾-point profit (60⅜-52⅝) while re-purchasing the put in the secondary market at a 4⅝-point (8⅛-3½) loss. The net result would be a 3⅛-point gain (7¾-4⅝). All calculations exclude transaction costs.

SUMMARY OF SIMPLE STRATEGIES

Simple Buying Strategies

For the put buyer, the first simple strategy (buying a put) provides a valuable vehicle to participate in the anticipated stock decline. In effect, it offers a limited-risk alternative to shorting the underlying stock itself which theoretically has unlimited upside exposure.

A put buyer would achieve the same gain (less the cost for the put) as a short seller, while limiting risk to no more than the cost of the put which normally accounts for only a fraction of what it would cost to buy the underlying stock.

Another simple strategy for the put buyer (buying stock, buying a put) is to combine buying a put with owning the underlying stock. In this strategy the put is used to protect a stock position either (1) already owned or (2) being acquired. In the first instance, the put is bought as an "insurance" against a possible stock-purchase mistake. In the second instance, the put is bought to protect an established stock position with large unrealized taxable gains which the stock owner is reluctant to realize the sale of the stock would produce.

Simple Selling Strategies

For the put seller, the simplest strategy (selling a put) offers a means of generating option-premium income or cash flow for his investment portfolio.

One sells (writes) a put on a stock one believes will rise in value. One expects to benefit from a stock rise which will render the put written worthless permitting one to keep the option without further obligations.

Another simple strategy (selling stock short, selling a put) for the put seller is to combine selling a put with selling stock short. If the stock price declines as anticipated, he will cover his stock position at a profit, reduced only by the cost of having to buy back the put written at a higher price. If the stock rises instead of declining, the option income will partially offset his loss in the short stock position.

Part II

PUT BUYING

Chapter 3

PUT BUYING: WHY & HOW

What:
A put buyer may or may not own the underlying stock. He pays the seller premium money for the *right* to sell stock.

Why:
Buying puts provides you with a means of investing small amounts of capital for possible higher returns. Also, along with a stock position, put buying gives you some protection for your stock position against possible near-term fluctuations in the marketplace.

How:
Buying puts alone gives you a chance to make money on a highly leveraged basis, while you couldn't lose more than the cost of your put. Buying puts and owning stock simultaneously would let your stock profit run at the relatively small cost of a put.

Three Important Reasons for Buying
Why should you buy the right to sell a security at a given price within a specified time period? There are several important reasons for doing so.

First, if you anticipate a particular stock is likely to decline in price, buying put options provides a way to profit from the decrease. A put buyer is allowed to participate fully in any decline in the price of the underlying security except for the initial premium paid for the put and, possibly, make substantial profits on a relatively small investment. Second, if you already own the stock and are reluctant to sell it at this particular time, the purchase of puts can provide protection—a "hedge"—against a substantial decline in its market price.

Third, if you are buying shares of an especially volatile stock, you may also wish to purchase puts as a way to establish a minimum selling price for the stock.

Risk Limitation
A put buyer will be required to pay the entire purchase price of the premium at the time of purchase. The premium paid for a put fluctuates with the market price of the underlying stock and the time remaining until expiration.

Although a put holder anticipates that the premium price will rise, it could decline. However, since he is under no obligation to exercise his right to sell the stock to the put contract seller (writer), his loss will be limited to the price paid for the put. He will lose his entire investment if he still holds a put when it expires. On the other hand, he may realize his loss at any time prior to expiration date by entering a sell order in the secondary market, or he can hold the option in the hope that its price will subsequently rise.

Similar vs. Dissimilar Aspects
In several aspects, the put buyer and the call buyer are similar.

First, as in call buying, the most frequent reason for buying puts is in anticipation of a significant moving in the underlying stock during the option's life, although the anticipated moves are in opposite directions. While the call buyer benefits when the price of the underlying stock rises significantly, the put buyer profits when the stock price declines sharply. This is because the value of a put rises as the stock price declines.

Second, like calls, puts are wasting assets and time works against the holder. The risk for both is limited to the amount paid for the option.

Third, as the case with a call holder, there is some salvage value for the put holder even if the market should go against him. Instead of allowing his put to expire unexercised, the holder might recapture part of his investment at any time prior to expiration date by entering a sell order in the secondary market, when there is still some time value remaining.

Put buying is different from call buying in one important aspect: the potential profitability is higher for the call buyer than for the put buyer. Whereas the reward for the call buyer is *theoretically* unlimited, the potential profitability of the put buyer is limited because the underlying security can decline only to zero. This distinction, however, is more theoretical than practical.

Covered vs. Uncovered Put Buying

A buyer of a put may or may not own the underlying stock. A put buyer who does not own the stock is said to be *uncovered* whereas one who owns the stock is said to be *covered*.

1. *Uncovered Put Buying*

When the stock is not owned, buying a "naked" put is the economic equivalent of shorting stock and buying a call, although the leverage is different with the two strategies. The maximum loss for the uncovered buyer is the premium paid. The gain on the position will move point-for-point with a stock that is falling in price below the exercise price.

2. *Covered Put Buying*

In the case where the stock is owned, the buyer of a put is taking out insurance against a long position. The investor who buys a put against long stock is in the same economic position as the buyer of a call option.

Put buying locks in a sale price but allows unlimited opportunity for gain (less the cost of the put). Purchasing the put permits the investor to ride through a short-term price decline in anticipation of long-term price appreciation.

Principal Uses

Put options are bought for a significant number of uses and with varying techniques. The two principal categories of put buying applications are:

1. Long Put
2. Long Put, Long Stock

Simply stated, "long put" is "uncovered" put buying while "long put, long stock" is "covered" or "protected" put buying.

Let's analyze, in some detail, these two principal put buying applications.

1. *Long Put*

Suppose you were the put buyer. You would agree to pay the put seller a certain amount of money, called the premium, in exchange for the *right* to sell him (put to him) 100 shares of a specified stock at a specified price at any point over a specified period. The last day of the contract period is called the expiration date, and if the op-

25

tion is not exercised before then, it is said to have expired.

You would get two things out of buying puts (A) leverage and (B) limited risk.

(A) Leverage

Buying puts can give you *leverage*, a means of investing small amounts of capital with the possibility of high
return.

Should the price of the underlying stock on which you
had bought a put decline over the life of the contract, the
option will become more valuable, and the premium will
increase. So it may be possible for you to sell the option
you have bought to another investor at a higher premium
than you paid for it.

A put could double or triple in value in a matter of
days with only a relatively small percentage decline in
the price of the underlying stock.

(B) Limited Risk

On the other hand, you could lose the entire premium
you pay for the put. To your advantage however, you
couldn't lose more than the cost of your put, and you
know the risk in advance.

Illustration

Assume XYZ stock was selling at 60 when you bought a January
60 put for 5. The following is an illustration of your profit and loss
results with the stock, at expiration, trading at different price
levels:

Stock Price At Expiration	Put Value At Expiration	Cost Of Put	Put Profit Or (Loss)
45	15	5	10
50	10	5	5
55	5	5	0
60	0	5	−5
65	0	5	−5
70	0	5	−5

If the underlying stock moves downward from 60 to 50, the put would have a value of 10, which, *less* the cost of the put (5), would produce a profit of 5 (disregarding commissions) for you. If the stock should fall to 45, the put value would rise to 15, which, *less* the cost of the put, would result in a profit of 10 for you.

On the other hand, a loss normally would occur if the stock should advance. The loss, however, would be limited to the cost of the put, regardless of how far the stock might go against you.

2. *Long Put, Long Stock*

The other principal purpose of put purchase is to protect an existing stock position as well as to generate income in uncertain or declining markets. Buying a put provides you with a vehicle, allowing you to let your profits run, while at the same time giving you some protection against possible near-term fluctuations in the marketplace.

Now, what would have happened if you'd been wrong and the stock had gone up rather than down? The premium you paid, of course, would be a loss. However, the put would have served its purpose by protecting you against potential major losses, while without unduly limiting further possible appreciation in your stock position.

Chapter 4

LONG PUT

What:
A "long put" is an outright put purchase without any hedge or "cover."

Why:
A "long put" is used (1) for outright speculation, (2) as a short-sale alternative, and (3) for protection.

How:
The put buyer should have an opinion not only about the *direction* and *extent* of stock market movement, but also about the *timing* of the movement.

While an out-of-the-money put costs less, its chance of becoming profitable is also relatively less. On the other hand, as in-the-money put costs more, but it has a better chance to attain profitability.

Three Main Applications
"Long put" is an outright put purchase without any hedge or "cover." It has three principal applications:
1. Speculation
2. Short-sale alternative
3. Protection

SPECULATION

The simplest use of a put purchase is for speculative purposes when the buyer hopes for a decline in the price of the underlying security in order for his put to become more valuable. More specifically, put buying should be considered by an investor seeking a highly leveraged, limited risk short position in a stock he believes will decline.

Illustration

Buy XYZ Oct 50 at 5 when XYZ is at 50.

XYZ Price At Expiration	Put Price At Expiration	Put Option Profit Or Loss
30	20	+ $1,500
40	10	+ 500
45	5	000
50	0	− 500
55	0	− 500
60	0	− 500

Since XYZ is at the strike price of 50, the price of $5 paid for XYZ Oct 50 is for the time premium.

Assuming that XYZ declines to 50 on the October expiration date, the put holder has the right to *sell* XYZ at 50—or 10 points above the market price. The put is said to have an intrinsic value of 10, that is, 50 (strike price)—40 (market price). As the put cost $5, the profit to the put buyer will be $5 ($10−$5) which will mean a profit of $500 ($5 × 100) per contract (100 shares).

If XYZ is at 45 when the put expires, the put would have an intrinsic value of $5 (50−45) which will mean breakeven for the put buyer since the put cost 5.

On the other hand, the put would have no intrinsic value if XYZ is at 50 or more on expiration date. Thus, any close above 50 for the underlying stock would mean a loss for the put buyer.

To recapitulate:

1. *If the stock price rises*

   If the stock rises above the strike price, the put will have no value to its holder (buyer). His maximum loss will be limited to the premium paid for the option. He may be able to reduce the loss by liquidating the put in the secondary market prior to expiration.

2. *If the stock price drops*

   If the stock declines below the strike price, the put

holder may either (1) sell the put in the secondary market, or (2) exercise the put by buying stock at the current market price and delivering it against payment of the higher exercise price.

SHORT SALE ALTERNATIVE

Another simple put application is as a short-sale alternative.

When an aggressive investor expects a stock to drop, he has a choice between shorting the stock and buying a put. Selling short and buying puts are two different means of achieving essentially the same objective. However, put buying has two major advantages over the short sale, namely: (1) leverage, and (2) limited risk.

1. Leverage

First, the put purchase provides leverage because of the much smaller initial investment.

A put buyer seeking to benefit from a decline in the stock price can do so with an investment that is equal to only a fraction of the cost required for shorting the stock itself. On the other hand, the short seller has to deposit a sizeable percentage (currently 50%) of the value of the underlying stock shorted.

If you were to short 100 shares of XYZ at $50, you would have to deposit a margin of $2,500 (50%). For the put buyer, his $500 option purchase price constitutes his entire cash layout.

Using the above prices for XYZ and its option on page 26, the following table compares short sale to put buying in terms of dollar and percentage profits and losses:

XYZ Price At Expiration	Short Sale	Put Purchase
30	+$2,000 (+80%)	+$1,500 (+30%)
40	+ 1,000 (+40%)	+ 500 (+100%)
50	0	− 500 (−100%)
60	− 1,000 (−40%)	− 500 (−100%)
100	− 5,000(−200%)	− 500 (−100%)

Illustration

Let's compare the two alternatives based on actual stock and put prices.

On June 15, 1977 with Avon (AVP) selling at 50¾ a share Investor A bought an Oct 50 put for $250. On the same day Investor B sold 100 shares of AVP short at 50¾.

Assume that when on September 15, 1977, AVP had declined 10 points from 50¾ to 40¾ Investor B could "cover" his short position at 40¾ (then market price) for a 10-point profit. Meanwhile, Investor A's Oct. 50 put probably would be trading at 11.

Let's compare the relative position of the short seller and the put buyer as follows:

	Investor B (Short Sale)	Investor A (Put Buying)
6/15/77	$5,075.00	$ 250.00
9/15/77	$4,075.00	$1,100.00
Profit before transaction costs	$1,000.00	$ 850.00
Initial investment	$2,537.50 (50%) margin)	$ 250.00 (put premium)
% Return on initial investment	39.4%	340%
Leverage	1	8.6

The leverage would be 8.6 to 1 in favor of the put buyer (340%) versus the short seller's 39.4%.

Had, of course, AVP not declined, or declined less than anticipated, the put buyer could have lost part or even all of the investment.

For practical purposes, let's use more illustrations of how a put buyer who anticipates a decline in the price of the underlying stock will earn a greater percentage return (leverage) on invested funds than if he sold the stock short.

31

Illustration

On June 17, 1977 General Motors was 69⅛ when an investor bought a GM Jan 70 put at 5. If, by September 15, 1977, GM had declined about 10% to 62, GM Jan 70 would probably be selling around 9, indicating a 4-point profit on a $500 investment (paid for the put).

On the other hand, had GM been sold short at 69⅛, the gain to the short seller would have been $712.50 ($6,912.50–$6,200.00) on an investment of $3,456.25 (margin deposit) over the same time period.

The comparison would be as follows:

	100 GM Shares Shorted	1 GM Jan 70 put bought
6/17/77	$6,912.50	$500.00
9/15/77	$6,200.00	$900.00
Profit (before transaction costs)	$ 712.50	$400.00
Initial Investment	$3,456.25	$500.00
	(50% margin deposit)	(put premium)
% Return on initial investment	20.6%	80.0%
Leverage	1	3.9

Thus, the leverage would be almost 4 to 1 in favor of the put buyer (80%) versus the short seller (20.6%).

The following is still another illustration of leverage comparison between put purchase and short sale.

On July 15, 1977 Eastman Kodak (EK) and its January 60 put closed, respectively, at 58⅜ and 4⅝. Assume an EK Oct 70 put was bought for $462.50 (4⅝ per share) by one investor while 100 shares of EK were sold short by another investor. About five months later, on Dec. 8, 1977, EK declined to 49¾, while EK Jan 60 put rose to 10⅛. Comparing the above two can be tabulated below:

	100 EK shares	1 EK Oct 70 put
7/15/77 stock sold short	$5,837.50	—
7/15/77 put bought	—	$ 462.50
12/8/77 short stock covered	$4,975.00	—
12/8/77 put sold	—	$1,012.50
Gross Profit	$ 862.50	$ 550.00
Initial investment	$2,918.75	$ 462.50
	(50% margin)	(put premium)
% Return on investment	29.6%	118.9%
Leverage	1	4

For those who wish to buy puts as an alternative to shorting a stock, it's important to understand the concept of what we call "depreciation factor."

The "depreciation factor" is designed to calculate by what amount the stock must decline for the percentage gain on the put at expiration to equal the gain on the shorted stock.

We use the following formula for such a calculation:

$$DF = (2M-S)/(M-P) \text{ minus } 1,$$

where "DF" is the "depreciation factor";
   "M" is the market price of stock;
   "S" is the strike price of a put;
   "P" is the put price.

Illustration

On June 21, 1977 Honeywell (HON) was selling at 54 and its Feb 50 put was trading at 1⅞. Applying the above formula, we have the following:

M = 54
S = 50
P = 1.875

$$DF = \frac{(2 \times 54 - 50)}{(54 - 1.875)} - 1 = \frac{58}{52.125} - 1 = 1.1127 - 1 = 0.1127.$$

The above means that the stock would have to decline 11.27% for a put purchase to offer the same percentage gain as could be achieved by shorting the stock.

A decline of this amount (11.27%) would cause the stock to fall to 47.914 (54 − 11.27% of 54). At that price, the 50 put is worth 2.086 (50 − 47.914) or a gain of 0.211 (2.086 − 1.875) over its 1.875 cost. This, indeed, is an 11.3% gain, thereby verifying the formula, and providing a quick answer to the short sale versus purchase of a put decision for capital gains.

2. Limited Risk

The second major advantage which put buying has over short sale is that whereas short sale has no limit to its risk on a price surge in the underlying stock, a put purchase has limited risk on the upside.

In addition to the above, the following are other advantages which put buying has over short sale.

3. No Margin Call

Unlike the short seller who is subject to margin calls if the underlying security should rise, the put buyer is free from margin calls.

4. Salvage Value

A put buyer can lose his entire investment if the price of the stock stagnates or rises during the option's life. However, he may be able to recoup some of his investment by selling the put in the secondary market for whatever value obtainable on account of its remaining life.

The same secondary market provides an outlet for a successful long put to be sold at a profit, or exercised, with the holder buying the stock at the lower market price and selling it at the higher strike price.

On the other hand, there is no salvaging outlet for short sellers in the form of a secondary market.

5. Flexibility in Timing

The short seller may be basically correct in his assessment about a particular stock. However, the stock might go up before it goes down. Should this happen, the short seller might be intimidated into covering the short at a loss.

On the other hand, since the risk to a put buyer is limited to the cost of the put, the assurance of limited risk gives the put holder more flexibility by making exact timing a less critical factor.

6. Instead of Stop-Loss Order

Related to the above timing factor is the role of a stop-loss order for the protection of a short position.

A stop-loss order is designed for the primary purpose of protecting a major portion of unrealized profits. However, while the stock might go down to a price level that would activate a stop order, the stock might then turn around and rise to new highs.

On the other hand, put buying provides a means of avoiding this latter possibility and insulating the stock from short-term breaks.

7. No Cash Dividend Liability

When a cash dividend is paid on the underlying stock, the short seller incurs a liability for that dividend.

On the other hand, listed options are not adjusted to reflect ordinary cash dividends.

Does a short seller have any advantage at all over a put buyer? The former does have one important advantage: If the underlying stock stands still, the time works against the put buyer, but not necessarily against the short seller.

PROTECTION

Shielding Profit

One use of puts is to achieve protection against an anticipated decline in the price of a stock you own and may not wish to sell for any number of reasons. For instance, you may not want to sell a stock which you may have acquired at a price level considerably below its current market value and, therefore, you are understandably reluctant to realize the large taxable gain that sale of the stock would produce.

One way to resolve this problem is to "lock" in most of the profit already made by buying a put whose strike price is near the then market value of the underlying security. Should a significant decline ensue, you have the right to sell the shares at the strike price, and thus protect your profit.

35

How The Protection Works

The protection works this way: By buying a put on such stock, any decline in the value of the stock should be largely offset by an increase in the value of the option. If the stock price increases, you will stand to benefit from the increase. There will be a serious tax problem, however, if the stock is held short term.

Illustration

Assume that on July 15, 1977 you had a substantial paper profit in Santa Fe International (SAF) which was selling at 53½ and you were reluctant to sell the stock even though you expect a possible decline in stock prices over the next several months. For protection, you bought an SAF Oct. 55 put at 3¼.

In three months, as of Sept. 14, 1977, SAF had dropped to 44 for a loss of 9½ on the stock. Meanwhile, however, as the stock declined in price, the put rose in value, possibly to the 10⅞ level. The 7⅜-point (10⅞−3¼) gain in the put served to offset somewhat the decline in the market value of the stock.

The Lesser Evil

In the event that the anticipated stock price decline doesn't materialize, you would only lose the price paid as an "insurance" for the put. In the above illustration on SAF, had the stock not gone down as feared, you would lose on the put. However, the relatively low cost of a put (3¼) would be the lesser evil than the indicated 9½-point loss on the stock.

Indeed, a stock may rise instead of going down as anticipated. The protection achieved by buying a put would serve to retain for you the opportunity to benefit from an increase in the price of the stock.

Illustration:

Assume that on June 10, 1977 you owned Revlon (RLM) at 38½ but were reluctant to sell the stock despite your bearish views over the near or intermediate term. You could buy a Sept 40 put at 3⅜ for protection.

As of Sept. 14, 1977, RLM, instead of declining, had risen 4¾ to 43¼ from 38½ while its Sept 40 put dropped $3^5/16$ (from $3^3/6$ to $1/16$). On balance, you would be better off because the $3^5/16$ point loss on the put would be more than offset by the 4¾-point gain on the stock.

Why Particularly For Volatile Stocks

As a protective device, puts provide a particularly useful investment tool in connection with speculative purchase of volatile stocks, because such stocks are especially vulnerable to downside correction.

To recapitulate, the use of put options enables you to limit your risk while reducing your opportunity for profit by only the cost of the put. Of course, when you expect a certain stock to go down, you could sell the stocks now in anticipation of being able to repurchase them later at a lower price. Even disregarding tax considerations, we prefer the alternate course of buying puts as an insurance, because the latter approach would involve less guesswork and less need to be precisely right in your timing. This gives you downside price protection while still retaining ownership of the stock and, with ownership, the opportunity to profit from subsequent appreciation in the price of the stock.

WHEN AND WHAT PUTS TO BUY

Choose Which Put To Buy

The put buyer must make the same decisions as a call buyer regarding which put to purchase.

Since, as a call, a put is an asset with a limited life, the put buyer should have an opinion not only about the *direction* and *extent* of stock price movement, but also about the *timing* of that movement. Timing should be a determining factor of whether you purchase a put in the less expensive, near expiration month, or in a more expensive, distant expiration month.

Also to be considered is whether you buy a put in-, out-of-, or at-the-money. This initial cost is larger for in-the-money puts because they have intrinsic value. Out-of-the-money puts cost less because they have no value other than the "time value."

Absolute Versus Relative Risks

As is the case with a call buyer, a put buyer can never lose more than the initial cost of buying the put regardless of how adversely the price of the underlying security may go against him.

To understand the risk ramifications of in-the-money and out-of-the-money puts, we use Honeywell (HON) as an illustration.

Illustration

On June 17, 1977, HON was selling at 53 and its Jan 45, Jan 50 and Jan 60 puts were selling at ¾, 2 and 8⅝, respectively, as tabulated below:

Jan 45	¾
Jan 50	2
Jan 60	8⅝

1. In-The-Money Puts

With HON at 53, in-the-money HON Jan 60 had an intrinsic value of 7 points and a time value of 1⅝ (8⅝−7). The stock had to move up at least 7 points by expiration date for this option to expire worthless. On the other hand, for an at-the-money or out-of-the-money put to expire worthless, it is only necessary for the underlying security to remain unchanged until expiration date.

On the minus side, absolute risk is larger with in-the-money puts relative to at- or out-of-the-money puts because changes in the premium of an in-the-money put are closely correlated with movement in the price of the underlying security. It is possible that the entire investment might be lost. In actuality, the whole amount probably will not be lost unless the stock moves up to the strike price of the put or higher. Indicative of this point is the above tabulation showing that, with HON at 53, its Jan 50 put was still worth 2 and even its Jan 45 still had a value of ¾.

2. Out-of-the-money

While the actual amount of money at risk with the purchase of an out-of-the-money put is relatively small, the risk of total loss is relatively large. This is because the likelihood of sufficient stock movement to make such an option profitable is relatively slim.

Since all of the value of an out-of-the-money option consists of time value, there is relatively little correlation between a move in the price of the underlying security and a change in the price of the option.

Above Or Below Strike Price At Expiration

What would happen to a put buyer if the price of the underlying stock on expiration date is (1) below the strike price, or (2) above the strike price.

1. What If Below Strike Price

If the stock were to decline well below the strike price of the put option, the put holder could make a profit. He could buy stock in the open market and then exercise his put to *sell* that stock for a profit at the strike price, which is higher.

2. What If Above Strike Price

On the other hand, if the stock were above the strike price of the put option at expiration, the put would expire worthless. No one would logically want to exercise a put option to *sell* stock at the strike price, which is lower than the market price.

TO SELL OR TO EXERCISE

Two Alternate Courses

For the holder of a profitable put, he can either (1) sell it in the secondary market or (2) buy the underlying security and exercise the put.

Generally, if a put (in-the-money) is selling for more than its intrinsic value, the put holder will realize more profit by selling his option than exercising it. The put holder can "exercise" his option any time during the put's life by simply buying the stock at the lower current market price and selling it at the higher strike price.

The following is a comparison of these two alternate approaches.

Illustration

On June 14, 1977, Honeywell (HON) and HON Nov 60 put were selling, respectively, at 52⅞ and 8. If, on Sept 15, 1977 HON had dropped 10% to 47¾, HON Nov 60 put might probably be selling around 15. Let's see what would happen under either of the two approaches.

1. If the Put Were Exercised

A stock purchase combined with the exercise of the put would have the following result:

Cost:	Put premium	$ 800.00
	Put commission	25.00

	Stock purchase	4,775.00
	Stock commission	80.00
	Total cost	$5,680.00
Proceeds:	Stock sale	$6,000.00
	Commission	100.00
		$5,900.00

Proceeds $5,900.00
Cost 5,680.00
Net Profit .... $ 220.00

2. If the Put Were Sold

The sale of the put in the secondary market would have resulted in the following:

Cost:	6/14/77 Put bought	$ 800.00
	+ Commission	25.00
	Total cost	$ 825.00
Proceeds:	9/15/77 Put sold	$1,500.00
	− Commission	50.00
		$1,450.00

Proceeds $1,450.00
Cost 825.00
Net Profit .... $ 625.00

The above profit of $625 realized from the resale of the put on the secondary market would be approximately three times the amount ($220) realized from the exercise of the put. There are two reasons for the larger realized profit from the resale of the put. For one thing, whatever time value remaining in the option would be lost to the put holder when the option is exercised. For another, option exercising costs much more in commissions than option resale in the secondary market.

Among factors affecting the decision to sell or exercise are transaction costs, margin requirements and tax considerations.

Third Approach

In addition to exercise or resale, a third approach is also available.

If a put holder remains bearish on the underlying stock, one alternative for him might be to "borrow" shares to deliver against his sales at the exercise price. In this manner, he creates a short position in the underlying stock (which must be appropriately margined) that he hopes to cover profitably by repurchasing the shares at lower prices in the future.

PUT BUYING AS TRADING VEHICLE

Locking In A Short-Sale Profit

After a substantial decline in the underlying security in which an investor had a short-sale profit, he might have difficulty deciding whether to cover the short or maintain the position.

Buying puts provides a means whereby the short seller would lock in his profit at a relatively small cost.

Illustration

On June 8, 1977, Eastman Kodak (EK) was selling at 60. Assume that an investor who had shorted EK at 75 earlier might decide to take his 15-point profit even if he felt EK might continue to fall.

One possible put strategy would be to cover the short and use part of the profits to buy an EK Oct 60 put for 3⅞. This put strategy would enable the short seller to take his profit and still participate in any further decline in the underlying stock, while his risk would be limited to the cost of the put (3⅞) plus transaction costs.

Averaging Down On A Short Position

The short seller in the above illustration might decide to add to his short position, instead of taking a 15-point profit.

41

One possible put strategy would be to buy EK Oct 60 at 3⅞, thus doubling his short position with an additional risk of only 3⅞ plus transaction costs.

Trading for Down Fluctuations

Under the protective umbrella of a put option, one can play the down fluctuations of the underlying stock.

This trading technique involves making a number of short-term transactions through buying the stock on dips and then selling the stock out on rallies. There is no limitation to the number of trades that can be made against a particular put during the life of the option.

Using Puts to Diversify

A bearish investor may use puts as a diversification vehicle. Diversification could be achieved by utilizing some of the funds earmarked for short stock to buy puts instead, because generally the cost of shorting a certain number of shares would be enough to cover many times that number through the use of puts.

In addition to greater diversification with the same amount of funds, such an approach also has several other important advantages: expanded downside leverage; risk limited to the money paid for the puts; and no margin calls if the underlying stock advances.

ALTERNATIVE RISK-MINIMIZING VEHICLE

Two Choices

Before buying puts, the investor must carefully weigh the cost and attributes of put options against alternative risk-minimizing vehicles.

While we mentioned briefly stop-loss orders as an alternative course to a put purchase, it is appropriate here to answer the frequently asked question: Why should an investor buy a put when a stop-loss order can provide similar downside protection without cost?

To begin with, let's see how a stop-loss order works. When an investor enters a stop-loss order, he instructs his broker to sell his long position "at the market" or "at a limit," as soon as the stock reaches a predetermined price.

Disadvantages

Compared to a long put position, a stop-loss order has a number of disadvantages.

1. No Flexibility

The put holder has more flexibility, since the put gives the holder the "option" to exercise, liquidate, or allow the put to expire, regardless of the underlying stock's fluctuations during the put's life.

On the other hand, after a stop-loss order has been entered, this order would become a market order when the price of the underlying stock reached the stop price. However, the investor would have no assurance that the stock would be sold at the exact stock price. In a sharply declining market, it is possible that the broker will be unable to execute the sell order until the stock has dropped substantially below the specified price. In contrast, the put holder is entitled to receive the contracted price for his stock upon exercise.

2. Untimely "stopped" Out

When the price of the stock falls to a predetermined level, your broker must "stop" you out. It often happens, however, that the stock's fall may be only temporary and could subsequently go back up. You may miss out on a large gain if the stock should go down to your stop-loss point, and then rebound to a much higher price. One who uses a stop-loss order to cut one's loss short is like going down to the "river of no return." In contrast, the put holder can afford to ride out a temporary storm because he can't lose more than the cost of the put.

3. Trading halt in stock

Execution of a stop-loss order may not be possible during such a market dislocation as a trading halt in the stock.

Advantages

A stop-loss order has several definite advantages over a long put. First, the former costs no money. Second, it has no fixed expiration date and can be maintained indefinitely, or "good 'til cancelled." Third, it can be used on an odd-lot (less than 100 shares) while listed puts generally cover 100 share units.

43

Sell-Stop

Let's examine another version of the stop-loss order which involves protection of profit.

Assume you have a paper profit of $1,500 in a stock after it had risen from 30 to 45. Further assume you are concerned about possible erosion of this paper profit. What would you do? You could sell the stock which, however, you may be reluctant to do, either for tax reasons, or for the expectation that the stock may have the potential for further gains.

One alternative for you would be to place a sell-stop order 5 to 10 percent below the market. This sell-stop order would accomplish the primary purpose of protecting a major portion of the profit. However, while the stock might go down to a price level that would activate a stop order, the stock might then turn around and rise to new highs.

Another alternative would be for you to buy a put which would provide the best means of avoiding this latter possibility and insulating the stock from short-term breaks.

Chapter 5

LONG PUT, LONG STOCK

What:
"Long put, long stock" means simultaneous ownership of both a put and its underlying stock.

Why:
This option strategy is primarily designed for investors seeking to limit the downside risk in a stock position during the life of the put.

How:
Under the cover of a protective umbrella (put), an investor may pursue his long-term growth possibilities in his stock position. Any increase in the price of the stock over and above the price paid for the put will result in a net gain.

Buy a Put, Buy Stock
When an investor simultaneously owns both common stock and a put on the same stock, he is protected against a possible substantial decline in the market value of the stock he either already owns or is buying. This "long stock, long put" strategy is designed primarily for an investor seeking to limit the downside risk of his long stock position during the life of the put.

For this downside protection, an investor pays a "protective" put premium which permits him to participate in a rise in the stock price. Any increase in the price of the stock in excess of the price paid for the put (plus transaction costs), will result in a net gain for the investor.

Protective Premium

While options are usually considered as short-term investment vehicles, put-buying, like call-writing, may actually allow an investor to pursue long-term investment strategies and to reduce his vulnerability to steep market corrections. Thus, for example, by buying puts, investors may maintain an existing position in long-term growth stocks in a depressed market, without being pressed into decisions regarding the disposal of such stocks.

Illustration

Assume that you had bought Mesas Petroleum (MSA) at 29⅝ on Oct 25, 1976. On Aug. 29, 1977 MSA closed at 42⅜. If you became concerned about possible erosion of your paper profit in an uncertain market, one means of defense would be to buy a Jan (5-month) 45 put at 4⅜.

If your concern proves groundless and the stock continues its upward course, you would simply allow the put option to expire. Your loss would be limited to 4⅜ as the cost of this protective premium, plus transaction costs.

On the other hand, should your concern about possible erosion of your paper profit prove to be well-founded, and the stock retreats to 30, you could exercise your put option and sell the stock at 45. Instead of having your paper profit completely wiped out, you would keep the bulk of that profit, namely 15⅜ minus 4⅜, paid for the put premium.

Complete Versus Partial Hedge

While covered call-writing offers a partial hedge against market decline, put buying provides the *only* method available in the option market whereby an investor can *completely hedge* a long stock position, assuming that the strike price of the put option is the same as the purchase price of the stock. This put hedge provides investors complete protection against loss regardless of how much the stock might decline.

Two Major Categories

This put strategy could be used for either:
    1. Protecting profits in a long stock position already established, or
    2. Hedging new long purchases.

In the first category, an investor is seeking protection for a long stock position (probably at a low cost) that he is not considering selling. In the second category, a stock buyer seeks "insurance" against possible mistakes.

PROTECTING EXISTING POSITIONS

Safeguarding Unrealized Profits
Put options can be purchased as a means of protecting unrealized profits in stock you own under two circumstances. First, you protect long-term capital gains in a stock you wish to hold indefinitely. Second, you freeze a capital gain or loss in a stock in the current year, and defer the tax consequences to the succeeding year.

This strategy applies when you are doubtful about the short-term prospects of certain stocks, but are still bullish about their long-term possibilities. Investors might also be reluctant to sell due to the resultant tax liabilities, especially for owners of stocks at a very low-cost basis.

If the investor is correct in his assessment about the underlying security, most of the long-term profits may be retained with the protection of a put. On the other hand, the loss to the put buyer would be limited to the premium paid for the put. Even such a loss might be reduced by liquidation of the put in the secondary market while it still had some remaining time value, and by the possibility of offsetting gains in the underlying stock itself.

The following are illustrations of buying puts to protect an unrealized profit in a long position already held.

Illustration
Assume that in middle 1976 an investor bought 100 shares of Penzoil (PZL) at 24⅞. On Jan. 19, 1977 PZL and its July 35 put closed at 34⅞ and 2½ respectively. He has a 10-point profit in his long position.

While the investor believed that the long term prospects for the stock were favorable, he desired to protect his unrealized profit against a possible short term decline by buying a July 35 put at $250 ($2.50 per share).

Let's see what would happen to the investor if the stock were to rise or decline for about 10 points.

47

1. What if PZL Rises About 10 Points

Should PZL rise to 45 by 1977 year-end, the investor will fully participate in the advance of his long position. The value of his put, however, will decline as the stock advances. In this event, he could allow the put to expire unexercised, or recapture some of the option premium paid by liquidating it in the secondary market. The profit in his long position cannot be reduced by more than the $250 paid for the option (disregarding transaction costs).

The above can be tabulated below:

	Stock Plus Put	Stock Only
Stock bought mid 1976	$2,488	$2,488
	($1,244 margin)	($1,244 margin)
Stock as of 1/19/77	$3,488	$3,488
Put bought 1/19/77	$ 250	
Stock as of 1977 year-end	$4,500	$4,500
Put as of 1977 year-end	0	
Profit	$1,762	$2,012
% Profit on investment	141.6%	161.7%

2. What If PZL Declines About 10 Points

Should the stock decline to 25, the investor could exercise his put by delivering his long stock against payment of the strike price ($35).

In this case his profit would be the $1,000 attributable to the long position, minus the $250 option premium, amounting to $750 (disregarding transaction costs).

No matter how much the stock might decline during the life of the put, the investor can exercise the put and deliver his long stock for $35 per share. He has thus effectively "locked in" a minimum $1,400 profit (disregarding transaction costs).

The following is another illustration for practice purposes.

Illustration

On June 3, 1977 Honeywell (HON) was selling at 50¼ and HON Oct 50 put was available at 2⅞. If an investor had bought

48

HON earlier at 44 and desired to protect his profits in the long stock position he could buy an Oct 50 put at 2⅞.

Let's see what would happen if the underlying stock were to either (1) rise 10 points or (2) decline 10 points.

1. Assume HON subsequently rises to 60¼—put expires and stock sold:

	Long Stock	Put
Stock bought (50% required)	$2,200	
6/3/77—Put bought (100% required)		$287.50
10/21/77—Put expires, stock sold	$6,025	
Profit or (Loss)	$3,825	($287.50)

2. Assume HON declines to 40¼—put is exercised:

	Long stock	Put
Stock bought (50% required)	$2,200	
6/3/77—put bought (100% required)		$287.50
10/21/77—Put exercised	$3,300	
Profit or (Loss)	$1,000	($287.50)

PROTECTING NEW PURCHASES

Establishing Minimum Liquidating Price

When an investor buys stock for appreciation purposes, he can buy puts to limit his risk in that long stock position. This "long stock, long put" strategy establishes a minimum price for the investor upon liquidating his stock, regardless of how severely the underlying stock may decline during the put's life.

The maximum loss in this strategy is limited to the cost of the put, less the amount realized, if any, from a closing sale of the put. Profits would result if the cost of the put is exceeded by the stock appreciation.

Illustration

On July 15, 1977, ABC Broadcasting (ABC) and its Feb 45 put had the following price data:

Strike Price	Put Price	Stock Price
45	2½	45⅞

Approximately five months later, on Dec. 8, 1977, ABC had declined 6⅛ (from 45⅞ to 39¾) while its Feb 45 put had risen 3⅞ (from 2½ to 6⅜).

1. *Long Stock Alone*

   If you were to long the stock alone, you would suffer a 6⅛-point loss.

2. *Long Stock Plus Long Put*

   If you combined a long stock position with a long put, you would offset the 6⅛-point loss in the stock with a 3⅞-point gain in the put, with an overall loss of only 2¼. To put it in even better perspective, the long put would eliminate 63.3% of the stock loss, leaving only 36.7% of the loss unprotected.

"Married Put"

A put bought simultaneously with the underlying stock is sometimes referred to as a "married put". The purpose of a "married put" is to reduce the downside risk inherent in owning the stock until the put expires.

The strategy of buying a put each time stock is bought is especially appropriate for tax considerations.

If an investor simultaneously buys a put and an equivalent amount of the underlying stock, and identifies the put as a "hedge" against the long stock position (i.e., to use such stock for delivery if the put is exercised), the holding period of the stock, for tax purposes, is not affected.

If the holding period of the stock is long term, it continues to be long term when the put is bought. If, however, the holding period of the stock is short term, the holding period of the stock is destroyed when the put is bought, and begins again when the long put position is closed out. Thus, if a stock had been held for seven months prior to the purchase of the put, the holding period of the stock would not begin anew until the long put expired or was sold.

If the hedge is set up and the put is allowed to *expire*, the cost of the put is added to the cost basis of the stock. If the hedge is broken by the *selling* of the put, the resultant profit (or loss) is a short term capital item.

LONG PUT, LONG STOCK VS. LONG PUT, LONG CALL

The following is a comparison between long put plus long stock on the one hand, and long put plus long call on the other.

Illustration

On June 10, 1977, Honeywell (HON) and its August 50 put and August 45 call had the following price data:

Strike Price	Call Price	Put Price	Stock Price
45	6⅞		51⅜
50		1⅜	51⅜

Long Put Plus Long Stock

Buy 100 shares HON at @ 51⅜ $5,138

Buy 1 HON Aug 50 put @ 1⅜ 138

Total Cost $5,276

This strategy permits retaining unlimited upside potential in the stock position, minus the relatively low cost of the put bought for protecting the stock position. On the downside, this strategy acts to limit possible setbacks in the stock price, while keeping its upside potential in the stock reduced only by the cost of the put.

Long Put Plus Long Call

Buy 1 HON Aug 45 call @ 6⅞ $688

Buy 1 HON Aug 50 put @ 1⅜ 138

Total cost $826

Note that the "deep-in-the-money" Aug 45 call is substituted for the long stock. Also note that the long call-long put combination costs only a fraction of what a combined long put-long stock position would cost.

This relatively low-cost strategy is designed for aggressive investors bullish on HON and seeking upside leverage.

(A) *Upside Breakeven Point*

For the investor to break even, the underlying stock would have to reach 53¼ per the calculation below:

HON call strike price 45

Cost of HON 45 call 6⅞

Cost of HON 50 put 1⅜

Upside break even point 53¼

(B) *Downside Protection Cost*

The cost of downside protection for this long put-long call combination is calculated below:

Upside break even point 53¼

less Put strike price 50

Cost of downside protection 3¼

Part III

PUT SELLING

Chapter 6

PUT SELLING: WHY & HOW

What:
We sell (write) a put by selling a put option on an underlying stock that we expect to rise in price or remain stable.

Why:
What we are shooting for is income, from receiving premium dollars, or, alternatively, acquiring, at a later date, shares below the current market price.

How:
We enter an order to sell a put option on a stock that we expect to rise; or, at the least, remain stable. This strategy is best suited to less volatile stocks.

POTENTIAL RISK AND REWARD

Put Writer (Seller)
When one sells (writes) a put, he is selling to another the right to sell a stock at the exercise price within a specified period of time. The seller (writer) must stand ready to buy the stock at the exercise or strike price any time during the option's life. Unlike the call writer, who must deliver stock and receive payment, the put writer delivers cash to pay for the stock purchase. For selling this right, he receives a premium.

Put option writers accept market risks on the downside. They take the risk that the stock might go down more than the premium received during the option's life.

Illustration

On Nov. 8, 1977, Avon (AVP) closed at 45 when its July 45 put was available at 3. If on that day you sold an AVP Apr 45 put and collected $3 per share (or $300 on a 100-share put contract) in premium money, you were said to be a seller (writer) of an AVP Apr 45 put at 3.

One possible motive for you to make that transaction was your expectation that AVP would probably remain stable or rise in price during the life of the put contract. If the stock does rise, you can realize a gain by closing out your position in the secondary market, or if the stock remains above the strike price, the put will expire so that you will pocket the premium money without further obligations.

ANALYSIS OF OBLIGATIONS

Meaning Of An Exercise Notice

If, however, on the other hand, the stock falls below the exercise price, you could be assigned an exercise notice. In that event, you would be required to buy the stock at the exercise price, which would be higher than the then market price.

While the put holder (buyer) normally will exercise only if the market price of the stock is below the exercise price, you (the put seller) should be prepared at any time to buy the underlying stock during the option's life. After the stock has been "put" to you through the exercise of the option by the put holder (buyer), you could immediately liquidate the stock and realize the loss, or hold the stock for possible future recovery.

Closing of a Purchase Transaction

The put writer need not remain obligated to buy the underlying stock throughout the option's life. He may cancel his obligation through a closing purchase transaction.

In a closing transaction, the option writer cancels his obligation by buying a put identical to the one previously sold. He will realize a profit if the cost of the put is less than the price at which he originally sold it, disregarding transaction costs. He will incur a loss if the cost of the put is greater than the price received.

The put writer will remain obligated until the option is liquidated, either through exercise, expiration or a closing purchase transaction.

COVERED VERSUS UNCOVERED PUT WRITING

The popular notion is that selling puts is speculative and, consequently, inappropriate for conservative investors. Actually, the word "conservative" carries different meanings for different individuals with varying investment motivations and objectives. Whether a certain option strategy is conservative or not depends on an investor's assessment of its relative risk and potential reward.

"Short Put" Versus "Short Put, Short Stock"

There are two types of put selling (writing): covered and uncovered. An uncovered put seller (writer) takes a simple "short put" position while a "covered" put seller (writer) combines a "short put" position with a "short stock" position.

The seller (writer) of an uncovered put is at risk if the price of the underlying stock declines, since he must, upon exercise, purchase the underlying stock at the exercise price, which will be above its current market price.

Even a covered put seller (writer) is substantially at risk. The term "covered" put writing is a sort of misnomer, because a "covered" put writer is only partially "covered," as his short position in the underlying stock is not completely hedged. If the stock price rises substantially, the writer may be forced to cover his short position by "buying in" the stock at a price much higher than the price at which he made his short sale.

Analysis Of Naked Put Selling

Strange as it may seem, selling a naked (uncovered) put places the seller in precisely the same economic position as if he were a "conservative" covered call writer. However, the leverage is different with these two strategies.

Assuming that the premiums for both a put and a call with the same exercise price and expiration dates are identical, the maximum downside risk is the same for the covered call writer who holds the underlying stock, as for the uncovered put writer who does not hold the stock.

The maximum risk for a call writer who buys a stock at 40 and receives a premium of 4 would be 36 (40−4), excluding commissions. The maximum exposure for an uncovered put writer who writes a put at 40 is likewise 36—the 40 he agrees to buy the

57

stock for if exercised, minus 4 he receives for writing the put.

Let's use an illustration to compare a naked put writer to a covered call writer.

Illustration

Assume XYZ is selling at 70, and its Jan 70 call and Jan 70 put are both trading at 4 ($400).

1. *The Opportunity and Risk Of A Covered Call Writer*

   Investor A buys 100 shares of XYZ at 70, and writes a Jan 70 call at 4 ($400). If XYZ stands still, or only moderately rises, he will earn $400; if it falls, he will lose the amount of the decline, less $400.

2. *The Opportunity And Risk Of A Naked Call Writer*

   Investor B sells a *naked* Jan 70 put at 4 ($400). If the stock stands still or rises, he will make $400. If the stock falls, he will lose the amount of that decline, less $400.

The following is another illustration of how uncovered put writing has essentially the same economic characteristics as those for covered call writing.

Illustration

On Nov. 8, 1977, Avon (AVP) had a July 45 put available at 3 when the stock was 45:

Strike Price	Put Price	Stock Price
45	3	45

Assume on that day you wrote a July 45 put, for which you received $300 (commissions excluded in illustrations). Now let's see how the passage of time, and changes in the price of the underlying stock would produce a number of possible results.

1. *What If The Stock Declined?*

   If the stock declined and the put were exercised, your account would be charged $4,500 for the purchase of 100 shares of AVP. However, your actual cost would be reduced to $4,200 per calculation below:

   Stock purchase cost ($45 × 100 shares) $4,500

   less put premium received ($3 × 100 shares) . . . . . ___300___

   Actual stock cost (before commissions) $4,200

2. *What If The Stock Rose?*

If the stock rose and the put expired, you would pocket $300 in put premium money without further obligations.

3. *What If You Closed Out Before Expiration?*

If, instead of waiting for an exercise by the other party (put holder), you closed out your written position by purchasing a July 45 put (identical to the one previously written), you would make money if the new put would cost less than the one previously written. You would lose money if the new put would cost more than the old one sold.

At the end of the option contract period, the approximate value of the put would be the amount the exercise price is above the stock price. In the above AVP illustration (with an exercise price of 45 for the put), the put should be worth 4 if the stock traded at 41, but worthless if the stock traded above the exercise price of 45.

The essential characteristics as revealed by uncovered put writing in our above illustration are the same as those for covered call writing. Just as for the covered call writer, the uncovered put writer would benefit if the underlying stock rose, although the latter achieved the result without owning the stock. If the stock should rise sufficiently for the call holder to exercise the option, he would sell his shares, while the uncovered put writer, with no exercise occurring, would not buy the stock.

In a declining market, the covered call writer would probably hold onto his stock, while the uncovered put writer would probably acquire the stock. The option money received from writing either the call or the put would have the effect of reducing the cost basis in both situations. Apparently, both writers would be adversely affected if the stock had a significant decline.

Risk Vs. Reward Potential

Let's use another illustration to compare, in more detail, an uncovered put writer with a covered call writer in terms of risk versus reward potential.

Illustration

For this illustration we will select a put and a call with *identical* premiums on a stock with the same exercise price and expiration month as follows:

Nov. 28, 1977 closing prices:

Continental Oil (CLL) 29⅞

CLL July 30 call 2

CLL July 30 Put 2

1. Risk-And-Reward Potential For The Covered Call Writer

Assume you bought 100 shares of CLL at 29⅞ and wrote a July 30 call for $200 ($2 × 100 shares).

If CLL stood still or rose slightly, you would earn $200. If CLL declined, you would lose the amount of the decline, less the call option premium ($200) received.

2. Risk-And-Reward Potential For Uncovered Put Writer

Assume you wrote a CLL July 30 put for $200 ($2 × 100 shares).

If the stock rose or remained unchanged, you would earn $200. If the stock fell, you would lose the amount of the decline, less the put premium ($200) received.

So you see that both the economic risk and potential reward of writing an uncovered put is essentially the same as writing a covered call.

Differences

What are the differences, then, between uncovered put writing and covered call writing?

1. Psychological Factor

One major difference is essentially psychological. Since the covered call writer already owns the stock, he is likely to be continually aware of the diminished value of his ownership if the stock suffers a sharp decline. On the other hand, since the put writer would not own the stock until an exercise takes place, it could come as a shock to him when the exercise happens, to pay $4,500 on a given day for 100 shares of stock worth only $3,500 on the open market.

2. *Initial Cash Outlay*

The covered call writer would have an immediate charge in his account due to the purchase of stock. On the other hand, a debit would not be created for the uncovered put writer unless the put were exercised.

3. *Cost Factors*

Cost factors tend to be lower for the uncovered put writer because there may be no stock commissions to pay. In the margin account there would be no interest to pay.

4. *Return On Capital*

The uncovered put writer would also tend to have lower margin requirements to back up the position. This could result in a greater return on the capital utilized.

HOW TO CHOOSE WHICH PUT TO WRITE

One writes (sells) a put option generally

1. To earn income and enhance his return on investment, and

2. To acquire stock at a cost below its current market value.

Choice of Exercise Price

The choice of exercise price will depend upon an investor's view of the underlying stock. If he is bullish, an investor might choose a put with a high exercise price and a larger premium, in anticipation of a rise in the stock value above the exercise price, in order to earn a greater return. Conversely, an investor might select a put with a lower exercise price so as to lessen the likelihood of exercise, or to acquire the stock at a lower cost in the event the put is exercised.

Let's use illustrations to compare what would happen to the put writer if the price of the underlying stock is below or above the strike price at expiration.

1. *If The Stock Is Below Strike Price At Expiration*

If the price of the stock subsequently declines below the strike price at expiration and the put is exercised, the put writer would be obligated to acquire the stock at the exercise price (higher than the then market price) less the premium received (disregarding transaction costs).

The result of this is to lower the effective price of the stock. His cost of acquiring the stock would be the exercise price less the put premium received.

Illustration

On March 16, 1977, Xerox (XRX) and its October 50 put closed at 50 and 4½ respectively. Assume that an investor sold a XRX Oct 50 put for $450 (4½ per share).

Near expiration, should XRX fall below the strike price of 50, the option would likely be exercised and the investor would have to buy 100 shares of XRX at $50 a share (higher than the market price).

If XRX declined to $47, he would have to pay $5,000 (plus transaction costs) for stock currently worth $4,700 in the market. His cost of acquiring the stock, however, would be reduced to 45½ a share, reflecting the $4½ per share premium. Were the stock decline substantial, e.g., to $40 a share, the put seller would be required to buy stock at $50 a share, incurring an unrealized loss (disregarding transaction costs) of $1,550 ($2,000 paper loss in his stock position offset in part by the $450 premium received).

It is apparent that puts should be written only on stocks that option writers would be willing to own.

2. *If Stock Is Above Strike Price At Expiration*

If the stock rises, as expected, above the strike price at expiration, and the option expires or is repurchased, the put writer will not acquire the stock. However, he would be compensated by an earned premium.

Illustration

In the above illustration on XRX, if the stock rises above the strike price of $50 by expiration, the option would probably expire and the put writer would earn the $450 premium (less transaction costs).

The put writer bases his transaction (writing) on his anticipation that the premium income (less transaction costs) will not be exceeded by the downside risk of the underlying stock.

PUT WRITING MARGINS

Different Margin Concept

The concept of covered writing is different for puts than it is for calls.

The put option writer will generally write against a cash margin. The put must be margined in the same manner as an uncovered call (i.e., 30% of the value of the underlying security:

Plus the amount that the put is in-the-money, or
Less the amount the put is out-of-the-money.

Margin Exceptions

The above margin requirement must be met unless one of the following conditions exists:

1. For margin purposes, a short put is deemed as covered only when the writer has, in his account, a long put on the same underlying security with a strike price equal to or greater than that of the short put.

2. No margin would be required of the writer if he has a letter of guarantee from an exchange approved bank, stating that funds in the aggregate amount of the strike price are on deposit at the bank.

Note: The Option Clearing Corporation will not accept bank guarantee letters on short stock positions. It is, therefore, up to each individual firm to decide whether it will accept a bank guarantee letter, in satisfaction of the firm's margin requirement.

WARNING: A put option writer holding margin will be subject to additional margin calls in a declining market, and be liable to pay for the stock in the event of exercise.

The importance of this point cannot be too over-emphasized, because some investors fail to fully understand put margining, and thereby fail to keep an adequate cash reserve behind each put they have written.

Chapter 7

SHORT PUT

What:
Also called "naked" put selling, "short put" amounts to selling puts against cash.

For selling a put, an investor takes the risk that the stock might go down more than the premium he receives from selling the put.

Why:
One sells a put primarily for receiving the option money, in the expectation that the put written will expire worthless if the stock declines as anticipated. One may also write a put in a stock one wishes to buy at a lower price.

How:
In return for having received the option money, the seller remains obligated to buy stock at the exercise price any time during the life of the option, should an exercise take place.

He would either earn the premium if the stock goes up, or buy the stock (at below-market price) if the stock goes down.

Writing Against Cash
What is a "short put"? It is "naked" or "uncovered" put writing as opposed to "covered" put writing. Whereas covered put writing "covers" a "short put" (an obligation to buy 100 shares of a specific stock at a specific price) with a "short stock", "naked" or "uncovered" put writing is not backed by a "short stock", but by cash or buying power reserves. Essentially, "short put" amounts to writing (selling) puts against cash.

Known vs. Unknown Risk
By writing a put and collecting the premium, you become obli-

gated to purchase the stock from a holder of the option if and when he decides to exercise his right to sell the stock. The price you will pay for the stock—if the put is exercised—is the exercise price specified in the option. This price will be higher than the market price.

The possibility of exercise is real for puts even if majority is distant. This exercise problem is far more serious with puts than with calls. Puts sell at parity faster and are exercised earlier for purely arbitrage reasons.

Unlike the uncovered call writer, whose risk is unknown, an uncovered put writer knows his downside risk—the worst that can happen to him would be that he would be required to buy the stock at the strike price. His effective cost of the stock will be the exercise price less the premium received from writing the option.

Since the possibility of being put is always present, the put writer is strongly advised to have enough reserve cash to pay for the delivery of the stock should the put option be exercised.

Be Financially Prepared

I would like to emphasize that writing puts on extremely volatile stocks can be quite dangerous. Since the put writer is responsible for paying the exercise price for the stock, the results can be disastrous if the underlying stock has dropped precipitously. Always prepare for the worst!

It is important to be financially prepared to buy stock if, as a result of a decline in the underlying stock, an exercise occurs. It would be a good idea to set aside enough money to buy a stock if the put is exercised. The money can be earning interest while you are prepared for this possibility.

Expecting A Rising Or Stable Stock

Generally you write (sell) a put on a stock that you expect to rise or, at the least, remain stable. If the stock stays above the exercise price, you will retain the option money received for writing the put.

STEP-BY-STEP WRITING PROCEDURE

Let's use an illustration to explain the step-by-step procedure of a typical put sale.

Illustration

On Nov. 25, 1977, Honeywell (HON) traded at 49½ when its May 50 put was priced at 3¾ as follows:

Strike Price	May 50 Put Price	Stock Price
50	3¾	49½

This is how we apply the put (selling) writing strategy:

Initial Put-Writing Position

Enter an order with your broker to sell (write) one HON May 50 put at 3¾ ($375) and thus establish your initial position:

Sell 1 HON May 50 put at 3¾ ($375)

Initial Margin Requirement

The initial put-writing margin requirement for most brokers is 30% of the stock value,
less the difference between the stock price and the exercise price if the stock sells above the exercise price, or *plus* the difference if the stock sells below the exercise price *reduced* by the amount of the put option received.

Calculation

100 shares of HON:
(100 × 40½ = $4,950)

30% of $4,950 ....$1,485

plus ½ (strike price: 50 −
stock price: 49½ .... $\underline{50}$
$1,535

reduced by the put premium ....$ 375
Initial margin required $1,160

The securities in your margin account may provide the collateral (initial margin) required to write a put.

Maintenance Margin Requirements

Maintenance margin requirements will increase or decrease as the stock declines or rises.

(1) What If The Stock Declines

Maintenance margin requirements will increase as the stock falls.

The requirement would increase $70 for each point decline in the stock, without considering the put premium received.

(2) What If The Stock Rises

Maintenance margin requirements would decrease $70 for each point rise in the stock, with a $250 minimum.

Potential Results at Different Stock Price Levels

The following is a tabulation of how your hypothetical put-writing position would stand, at expiration, with the stock at different price levels:

Stock Price Levels	May 50 Put Value	Gain/(Loss) on the put
52	0	$375
51	0	375
50	0	375
49½	0	375
48	$200	175
47	300	75
46¼*	375	0
45	500	(125)
44	600	(225)
43	700	(325)

*Breakeven level (with put bought to close out position)

Option Profit Levels

Conversely, a put decreases in value as the stock increases in value.

As you can see from the above tabulation, if the stock is trading above the put's exercise price at expiration, the put will expire worthless. You benefit from retaining the put premium received from writing the put.

67

When And How To Close Out

If the stock declines sharply below the exercise price, consider closing out your put option to prevent exercise. You may terminate your option obligation at any time so long as the put holder (buyer) hasn't exercised the option.

You close out by purchasing a put identical to the one previously sold. If the closing costs are higher than the premium originally received, a loss will occur. On the other hand, a gain will result if closing costs are lower than the premium received.

If the put holder exercises the option (with the exercise price higher than the stock price), you will acquire the stock. However, the effective cost for your stock acquisition will be the exercise price, *less* the option premium received as follows, per our above illustration:

Exercise price on HON May 50 put 50
less put premium received from writing the put . 3¾
Stock cost before commissions 46¼

No exercise will take place unless the exercise price is above—perhaps substantially above—the stock's current market value. If no exercise takes place, you will have earned premium income as a return on the cash in your investment account.

Not That "Naked"

"Naked" put writing is more conservative than it indicates. It may prove to be a more attractive conservative investment technique than covered call writing, which has gained wide recognition by institutions and regulatory authorities as a prudent, conservative investment approach.

The put writer accepts a considerable risk should the price of the underlying security decline. For what objectives, then, would an investor want to write a put?

Put options are written (sold) for a significant number of purposes, including two principal ones:

1. To Earn Premium Income

An investor may write (sell) a put option to earn premium income on the expectation that the put option written will not be exercised (expiring worthless). He writes the put as a means of increasing his cash flow, when he is reasonably sure that the underlying security will be either at or above the strike price during the life of the option.

2. *To Buy Stock at Below-Market Price*

An investor may write (sell) a put option as a means of acquiring a stock at a below-market price. Such an investor enters into an uncovered put option contract with the anticipation that a future price decline may occur, permitting the writer to buy the stock, during the life of the contract, at a cost lower than the current market price.

TO EARN PREMIUM INCOME

Adding to Dividends

One reason for writing put options: to increase the cash flow from your investment portfolio. Option premiums can add substantially to your income from dividends and other sources.

If you are looking for premium income, generally you would write puts in advancing markets just as you would write calls in declining markets. In other words, you would sell a put on a stock you believe will probably rise in price.

Two Ways of Earning Premium Income

You may realize premium income in one of two ways. One way is for the underlying stock to advance and for the put to expire worthless. Another way is to repurchase the put on the secondary market at a profit.

The put seller will earn the premium income when the price of the underlying stock is either (1) flat or has a moderate rise or (2) has a significant rise. In the first instance, the put you have sold will expire worthless. In the second instance, the put you have sold could be repurchased at a lower price than the price you paid. In either case, a profit will result for you.

On the other hand, a decline in the price of the underlying stock would cause a rise in the value of the option and a probable loss to you. You will have to either repurchase your put at a higher price in the secondary market to terminate your obligations, or take the stock "put" to you by the put holder at a price higher than the market price.

Let's see how a "short put" would work for you in producing premium income in one of the two ways: (1) to expire worthless:

and (2) to be repurchased at a profit in the secondary market.

(1) Expire Worthless

Anticipating a flat or moderate rise in the underlying stock, the uncovered put writer sells (writes) a put option, seeking to profit from a dissipation of the option time value. In other words, the put writer expects the following two developments to occur: (1) failure for the underlying stock to decline much below the exercise price, and (2) dissipation of option time value. His bet is that the put option written will not be exercised (expiring worthless).

Illustration

On June 8, 1977 when Eastman Kodak (EK) was selling at 60, EK Jan 60 put could be written for 4⅞. If on expiration date EK were above the exercise price of 60, the put would expire worthless, and the put writer (seller) would retain the premium originally received.

(2) Profitable Repurchase At Secondary Market

Sometimes you needn't wait until the expiration of the option to realize your profits, if the underlying stock should rise as anticipated. With an increase in the price of the stock, the value of the put you have sold would decline. Thus, you could buy an identical put option (closing transaction) in the secondary market at a lower cost than you received from the sale of the put (opening transaction).

Illustration

In the above illustration on EK, if the stock subsequently rose to 64, EK June 60 might be selling for 1⅜, at which point it could be repurchased for a profit of 3½ points (4⅞ − 1⅜) before transaction costs as follows:

EK Jan 60 put bought back at 4⅞
EK Jan 60 put originally sold at 1⅜
       Profit 3½

With the passage of time, sometimes even a relatively small rise, or no action in the price of the underlying stock, would produce a profit for the put writer due to the "wasting asset" feature of options.

TO ACQUIRE STOCK AT BELOW MARKET PRICE

Why Not Pay Less?

Sometimes you can get away with not paying the existing market price of a stock which you would like to own.

Put writing provides a possible means to buy a certain stock at a below-market price for investors who are seeking to buy the stock, but are unwilling to pay the current price.

Establishing An Effective Cost

Here is how it works. You may write a put on an underlying stock in expectation of acquiring that stock at a lower price if the put is exercised and "put" to you. Your cost of owning the stock would be the exercise price, less the premium received for writing the put. Stated in another way, by writing a put option you establish your effective cost of the stock—if the option is exercised—at the exercise price minus the premium received for writing the option.

On the other hand, if the put is not exercised, you will not acquire the stock but will still retain the premium.

Here is an illustration of this buy-below-the-market method of writing (selling) an option against *cash*.

Illustration

On June 22, 1977, Sante Fe International (SAF) was selling at 53¼. You might want to buy SAF, but felt the stock was priced too high. You would not buy SAF unless it dropped to the 48 level. With this view, you bought a SAF Jan 50 for 2⅛.

If the stock should fall below the strike price of 50, the put holder most probably would exercise the option and "put" the stock to you as the put seller (writer). In that event the effective cost for you to acquire SAF would be 47⅞ (50−2⅛) plus commissions. The put premium of 2⅛ received would have the effect of reducing your purchase price by that amount.

On the other hand, if SAF rose in price, the put would not be exercised. While you would not acquire the stock you would retain the premium upon expiration.

Key Consideration

In other words, as the put writer you would either earn the

premium if the stock goes up, or buy the stock (at below-market price) if the stock goes down.

Since the put seller may be forced to buy the stock if the put is exercised, he should only sell a put in stocks he would in any event be willing to own. Thus, one of the key considerations in put writing is whether or not the put writer (seller) desires to own the underlying stock and, if so, at what price.

Another Method of Lowering Purchase Price

Another option strategy to lower the effective cost of acquiring a particular stock is one involving writing puts with different strike prices or different expiration months. The following is an illustration of such strategy using different strike prices.

Illustration

On Nov. 10, 1977, you might want to acquire 200 shares of Santa Fe International (SAF) at a price lower than its then market price (49).

One SAF July put with an exercise price of 45 (out-of-the-money) might be written for a premium of 2¼, and another SAF July put with an exercise price of 50 (in-the-money) might be written for a premium of 4⅝. The average premium would then be 3⅞ as follows:

SAF July 45 put	2¼
SAF July 50 put	4⅝
Divided by 2	3 7/16

Let's see what would happen to you as the put writer if the underlying stock should (1) go up; (2) remain unchanged; or (3) go down.

(1) What If The Stock Rises?

Should the stock go up, you would not acquire the stock, but would be able to retain the entire premium amount of 6⅞.

Failure to acquire stock doesn't mean you can't subsequently use the cash in your account—which has now been increased by the option premium (6⅞)—to purchase the stock in the market. As long as the market price of the stock is less than 42⅞ (49−6⅞) a share, you would be better off having written the option (rather than buying the stock without obtaining option premiums as a means of reducing your purchase price).

(2) What If Stock Remains Unchanged?
    Should the stock remain unchanged at 49, the put with the exercise price of 50 would be exercised, giving you an effective purchase price for 100 shares of 45⅝ (exercise price of 50 less the premium of 4⅜). The remaining put would expire worthless, allowing you to retain the 2¼ in premium.

(3) What If The Stock Goes Down?
    Should the stock fall below 45, then you would have to buy 100 shares at 50 and 100 shares at 45, for an average price of 47½ as follows:

Buy 100 shares @ at 50
Buy 100 shares @ at ....<u>45</u>
$$95$$

Average purchase price
  (divided by 2) 47½

On the other hand, the average premium of $3^7/_{16}$ would lower the effective purchase cost to $44^1/_{16}$ ($47½-3^7/_{16}$), which is $4^{15}/_{16}$ points ($49-44^1/_{16}$) below the initial market price of 49.

Investment Flexibility
Although put writing obligates you to purchase the underlying stock if and when the option is exercised, this obligation can usually be terminated at any time prior to exercise simply by buying in the put. That is, by purchasing an identical put, and thereby offsetting the obligations of the one previously written.

Whether this results in a profit or a loss will depend on whether the premium paid (to buy in the option) is lower or higher than the premium originally collected.

In either case, the opportunity to offset an outstanding option results in investment flexibility—the opportunity to change your mind if and when circumstances change.

Illustration
Assume that on June 10, 1977, you collected 3¼ per share on writing a Dec 55 put option on Northwest Industries (NWT)

which was selling at 57, indicating that you probably would be willing to own NWT shares if they could be purchased at 51¾ (55 − 3¼).

On Sept 14, 1977, NWT declined to 52½. Since the option still had about three more months remaining until expiration, its holder might have not yet exercised it. Meanwhile, if you as the put writer (seller) decided that you were no longer interested in owning NWT stock, or at least not at the exercise price of 55, you could terminate your obligations under the option by buying in the put previously written.

If the then put price was less than 3¼ per share, you would realize a profit, exclusive of commissions and taxes. If it was more than 3¼, you would incur a loss.

Since an offsetting NWT Dec 55 put could be bought at 4, you would have suffered a loss of ¾ (4 − 3¼) before transaction costs as follows:

NWT Dec 55 put bought back at 4
NWT Dec 55 put originally sold at 3¼
Loss .... ¾

In-The-Money Versus Out-Of-The-Money Put Writing

For an easy explanation of the relative pros and cons of in-the-money versus out-of-the-money put writing, let's take a look at the following three July puts of Mesa Petroleum (MSA) on Nov 11, 1977, when MSA closed at 40⅞:

Strike Price	Put Price	Stock Price
35 (out-of-the-money)	1⅜	40⅞
40 (near-the-money)	2¾	40⅞
45 (in-the-money)	5¼	40⅞

1. In-The-Money Puts

Normally a 45 put, being in-the-money 4⅛ (45 − 40⅞) with the stock at 40⅞, is most likely to be exercised, unless the underlying stock rose above the strike price of 45 before expiration. While the risk of exercise is greater with in-the-money puts, they offset such risk by providing more premium income.

In the case of high-volatility stocks such as MSA, however, the chance of its rising above the strike price of 45 is real, with the resultant possibility that the put buyer may not exercise the option.

2. *Out-Of-The-Money Puts*
   Normally a 35 put, being out-of-the-money 5⅞ (40⅞−35) with the stock trading at 40⅞, is most unlikely to be exercised, unless the stock declined below the strike price of 35. Thus, writing out-of-the-money puts reduces the risk of exercise but, at the same time, the amount of available premium income.

MULTIPLE-EXERCISE-PRICE PUT WRITING

Different Exercise Prices
You may write puts with different exercise prices instead of writing puts with a single exercise price.
   Illustration
   On Nov. 25, 1977, Mesa Petroleum (MSA) had the following Jan 40 and 45 puts when the stock was 44:

Strike Price	Put Price	Stock Price
40 (out-of-the-money)	1¾	44
45 (in-the-money)	3⅞	44

Assume you sold a 40 put for 1¾ and a 45 put for 3⅞:
Sell Jan 40 put at 1¾
Sell Jan 45 put at 3⅞

Total premium received 5⅝
Average premium
(divided by 2) 1¹³/₁₆

Next, let's see how you would be doing if the stock should (1) rise; (2) stand still; or (3) decline.

1. *What If The Stock Rose In Price?*
   Should the stock rise above the higher strike price of 45, you would pocket the entire premium of 5⅝ without further obligations.

75

2. *What If The Stock Remained Unchanged?*

If the stock should stand still at 44,

(1) the 40 put would expire worthless, permitting you to retain the premium of 1¾ on the 40 put without further obligations.

(2) the 45 put would be exercised, forcing you to buy 100 shares of stock at an effective purchase price of 41 per following calculation:

Buy stock at exercise price of 45 45
less premium received from writing
    the 45 put . . . .<u>4</u>

Effective purchase price 41

3. *What If The Stock Fell In Value?*

Should the stock decline below the lower strike price of 40, the put writer would be compelled to buy 100 shares at 45 and another 100 shares at 40, for an average price of 42½, per calculation below:

Buy 100 shares at 45
Buy 100 shares at . . . .<u>40</u>

                                            85

Average purchase price
    (divided by 2) 42½

The average purchase price of 42½, however, would be reduced by the average premium received to $39^{11}/_{16}$ per the following calculation:

Average purchase price at 42½
less Average premium received . . . . $2^{13}/_{16}$

Average effective cost
    (excluding commissions) . . . .$39^{11}/_{16}$

Thus, the average effective cost of $39^{11}/_{16}$ would be $4^5/_{16}$ below the initial market prive of 44 per calculation below:

Initial market price 44
less Average effective cost . . . .$39^{11}/_{16}$
                                           $4^5/_{16}$

HOW TO MEASURE VOLATILITY

When you select a stock to write puts, you should be aware of its volatility history, because its tendency to move wildly could spell disaster for you. Volatility is a statistical measure of a stock's tendency up and down, based on its price history.

Meaning Of Beta

A stock's price movement volatility is also called Beta which is its propensity to move with the market. Generally, a stock with a higher Beta will most likely move *up* or *down* faster and further than one with a low Beta.

It is impossible, at least for the short duration of a stock option, for anyone to accurately predict the price movement of the stock. We have yet to find one who can. However, it is very possible to predict whether a particular stock is likely to have a large or small price movement, based on its historical performance. Certain stocks, throughout many years, have always moved *up* or *down* sharply relative to the market as a whole, and these stocks are very likely to do so again.

Which Direction? To What Extent?

The importance of the Beta of a stock to successful stock option trading cannot be over-emphasized. One of the overiding questions for a buyer or seller of an option (whether call or put) is whether its underlying stock will go up or down during the period of the option, and if it does, by how much, or to what extent.

In determining the answer to this question, the behavior of the stock price movement in the past is invaluable. And the stock with the likelihood of greatest movement (either up or down) has the highest Beta. Therefore, generally the buyer (whether call or put) should seek a stock with a relatively high Beta. On the other hand, generally the seller (whether call or put) should seek a stock with a relatively low Beta.

Key Consideration

Since the put seller may be forced to buy the stock if the put is exercised, he should only sell puts in stocks he would in any event be willing to own. Thus, one of the key considerations in initiating put selling (writing) is whether or not the seller desires to own the underlying stock and, if so, at what price.

If the stock price falls below the sum of the put exercise price and the premium received, the seller's loss could be point to point with a sharply declining stock.

MEANS OF DEFENSE

Concept Of Defense

Most options are written by sellers who have, or will immediately establish, a concurrent stock position to offset the option in the event that it is exercised. This means of defense is available both to call and put sellers (writers), as follows:

Short put, Short stock (sale of put vs. short position in the stock)

Short call, Long stock (sale of call vs. long position in the stock)

Some writers prefer selling options without the protection of an offsetting stock position in their accounts. They believe that the odds are on their side. Securities & Exchange Commission inquiries in the 1960s revealed that only one-third of all options written were ever exercised, and only 20 percent were fully profitable for the buyers. This means that two-thirds of the time, a naked option writer would have profited by keeping all or part of the premium he received without undertaking a stock position during the life of the option contract.

Basic Ground Rules

What are the possible defenses for put option writers to minimize their exposure? To begin with, there are several basic ground rules to observe:

1. Sell put options only against cash and only on securities for ownership

2. Use only a fraction of your funds in any single put option writing situation.

3. Place a ceiling on the number of put options sold to expire in any one month. This spreads risk and evens out fluctuations.

Defense Strategies Against Adverse Stock Action

Specifically, there are several defense strategies for the put option writer if the underlying security upon which he has issued a put option has declined in price.

Defense #1: Naked Call Writing

One possible recourse open to the writer who remains bullish about the stock in spite of its price decline is to write a naked call option at the price to which the stock has declined.

Defense #2: Selling Stock Short

Another possible recourse is to sell the stock short at a price to which the stock has declined.

Defense #3: Selling Stock Short Plus Call Buying

A third possible defense is to sell the stock at the price to which it has declined, and to purchase an above-the-market call at the original strike price for the remaining period of the put option. This defensive strategy is to limit loss of the premium paid for the above-the-market call, as well as to prevent substantial loss. This strategy is suited primarily for professionals instead for the average investor.

To recapitulate: Writing (selling) puts is to obtain premium income; also it offers a way of possibly acquiring shares of stock at below its current market price.

In the first instance, if the underlying stock should go down instead of going up as anticipated, the put holder would exercise the option. Thus, the put writer (seller) must be prepared for the possibility of paying far more for the stock than its current market price. This fact is one of the most important factors in evaluating the risks of put writing. In the second instance, a rise in the price of the underlying stock would compensate the put writer (seller) with the opportunity to buy the underlying stock at a below-market price, provided that the stock is the one he would like to own in the first place, albeit at a lower price. If the stock did not go up, the put writer would be compensated by retaining the premium received.

Chapter 8

SHORT PUT, SHORT STOCK

What:
"Short put, short stock" is an option strategy which combines selling a put with selling short on the underlying stock.

Why:
The objective for this "dual short" strategy is that if the stock price should decline as anticipated, the investor could cover his short stock position at a profit and repurchase his put at a loss, with an overall gain for the two transactions.

How:
This dual position is protected on the upside only to the extent of the premium money received. A loss would occur if the stock rises substantially instead of the anticipated decline.

HEDGED PUT WRITING

Only Partially Covered
As distinct from "uncovered" put writing, "covered" put writing combines a "short put" with a concurrent "short stock" position. Actually, the term "uncovered" put writing is a sort of misnomer, because a "covered" put writer is only partially "covered", as his short position in the underlying stock is not completely hedged.

This position is protected on the upside only to the extent of the premium received from the sale of the put. If the underlying stock rises substantially, the "covered" put writer may be forced to cover his short position by "buying in" the stock at a price much higher than the price at which he made his short sale.

High-Risk Bear Strategy

This is a highly risky strategy because there is the possibility of unlimited losses if the stock should rise in price and, therefore, is suitable only for the sophisticated investor able and willing to assume a large risk.

The "short put, short stock" strategy is to short the stock and write a put against the short stock position. This is a bearish put strategy.

A put writer is not required to deposit margin if he has a corresponding short position in the underlying security.

Let's see how this "short put, short stock" strategy would work if the underlying stock should (1) decline as expected or (2) rise instead of declining as anticipated.

1. If Stock Declined

If the stock price should decline as anticipated, the investor could cover his short stock position at a profit and re-purchase his put in the secondary market at a loss. He would realize a gain if the short-stock-sale profit exceeds the loss on the put sale, or a loss if the profit from the short stock sale is less than the loss from the put sale.

Illustration

On Sept. 2, 1977, Eastman Kodak (EK) traded at 61⅜ when its Apr 60 put was 3½. An investor sold 100 shares of EK at 61⅜ and, simultaneously, sold an Apr 60 put for 3½ ($350.00).

As of Nov. 25, 1977, EK had declined to 53 while its Apr 60 put had risen to 7½.

The investor could realize a gain of 4⅜ by covering his short stock position at a 8⅜-point profit and repurchasing the put in the secondary market at a 4-point loss:

	Stock	Put
9/2/77　Stock sold short at 61⅜ ...	$6,137.50	
9/2/77　Put sold at 3½	.....	$350.00
11/25/77　Stock covered at 53	$5,300.00	
11/25/77　Put repurchased at 7½ ...	....	$750.00
Gain or (loss)	$ 837.50	$400.00
less	400.00	
Net gain before commissions	.$ 437.50	

Or, he may choose to wait to receive an exercise notice, and use the stock "put" to him to cover his short stock position. In that event, his profit would be the premium originally received upon sale of the put.

2. *If The Stock Rose*

If the stock should rise instead of declining as anticipated, the investor would still be hedged to a certain extent, since the premium income from the put will partially offset his loss from his short position.

Illustration

On Sept. 2, 1977, Sante Fe International (SAF) traded at 46⅝ when its Apr 50 put was 5½. Assume an investor, applying the "short put, short stock" approach,

Sold 100 shares of SAF short at 46⅝
Sold One SAF Apr 50 put at 5½

As of Nov. 28, 1977 SAF had risen sharply to 53½ instead of declining as anticipated, while its Apr 50 put had dropped to 1⅞. The investor could take an aggregate 3¾-point loss by covering the stock at a 6⅞-point loss, and repurchasing the Apr 50 put at a 3⅛-point gain:

	Stock	Put
9/2/77		
Stock sold short at 46⅝ ...$4,662.50		
9/2/77		
Put sold at 5½		$500.00
11/28/77		
Stock covered at 53½ $5,350.00		
11/28/77		
Put repurchased at 1⅞ ...		$187.50
Gain or (loss) ....$ 687.50		$312.50
less 312.50		
Net loss before		
commissions ....($ 375.00)		

Thus, the investor would offset his short-sale loss of $687.50 with a put-sale gain of $312.50, resulting in a net loss of $375.00 before commissions. On the other hand, a short seller without the risk-reducing factor of the premiums received from writing a put would suffer his entire short-sale loss without any offsetting gain.

HOW TO SELECT THE STRIKE PRICE

Considerable Flexibility

Options of different strike prices provide investors with considerable flexibility in tailoring a strategy that best conforms to their specific market view and investment objectives.

Here is a summary of how investors use options (1) at-the-money, (2) in-the-money or (3) out-of-the-money when they establish, concurrently, a "short put" position and a "short stock" position.

1. At-The-Money

On Nov. 8, 1977, Avon (AVP) traded at 45 when its July 45 put was 3:

Strike Price	Put Price	Stock Price
45	3	45

Let's see what would happen to the investor if the stock (1) remained unchanged; (2) declined; or (3) rose.

(1) What If The Stock Remained Unchanged?

The maximum profit would occur if the stock remained unchanged at expiration date. The investor would be even in the short stock position while the 45 put would expire worthless, permitting the investor to retain the entire premium money of $300 (3).

(2) What If The Stock Declined?

If the stock dropped 5 points to 40, the put holder would exercise his option. The investor would use the stock thus acquired upon exercise to close out the short position. The 5-point gain from the short sale would be partly offset by the 3-point loss in the put sale.

(3) What If The Stock Went Up?

If the stock rose, say, 5 points to 50, the 5 point loss in the short stock position would only be offset to the extent of the 3 point premium received from the put sale.

2. In-The-Money

An in-the-money put might be used when the investor anticipated that the stock might be strong over the near

83

term, and was concerned primarily with as much upside protection as possible.

Illustration

On Nov. 25, 1977, General Motors (GM) traded at 66 when its July 70 put was 6¼:

Strike price	Put Price	Stock Price
70	6¼	66

If the investor were to sell 100 shares of GM at 66 and, simultaneously, sell one GM 70 put for 6¼, his potential results would be as follows:

(1) If The Stock Is Below The Strike Price

If the stock closed below the strike price of 70 at expiration, the put holder would exercise his option. The effective purchase price for the investor would then be the exercise price (70), less the premium (6¼) received, amounting to 63¾ (70−6¼)

This put would provide upside protection since the investor would not lose money unless the stock sold above 72¼ at expiration per calculation below:

Stock price 66
plus Put premium received......................6¼

72¼

3. Out-Of-The-Money

On Nov. 25, 1977, Eastman Kodak (EK) traded at 53 when its July 50 put was 2½:

Strick price	Put Price	Stock Price
50	2½	53

The investor would not have to buy the stock unless it declined below 50 at expiration. If this happened, and the put was exercised, the effective purchase price would be 47½ per calculation below:

Put strike price............................50
less Put premium received 2½

47½

He would lose money at any stock price levels above
55½ per calculation below:

Stock price 53
Plus Put premium received...................... 2½
                                              ————
                                               55½

Thus, very little upside protection would be provided
by the sale of this put.

Chapter 9

SHORT PUT, LONG STOCK

What:
"Short put, long stock" involves selling a put against a stock which he either owns or would like to own at a lower price.

Why:
The put seller is bullish to neutral on the underlying stock which is expected to rise in value.

How:
If the stock appreciates as anticipated, the put seller will be able to keep the premium money without further obligations. As long as the stock remains stable or rises, he will pocket the money.

Writing Either With Or Without Stock Ownership
An investor may write puts against a long stock position which he either (1) already has or (2) wouldn't mind having at a lower price.

In the first instance, he is bullish on the market in general and on the underlying stock in particular, and believes that the put will most likely not be exercised, as the underlying stock will appreciate, and be above the exercise price at expiration. Writing puts against stock owned may be viewed as a way to increase the cash flow on a position which is being held for long-term appreciation. As long as the stock remains at the same price or goes up, the writer will keep the premium.

In the second instance, he is bullish to neutral on the underlying stock and considers the sale of a put as an alternative to the use of a limit buy order. A limit buy order is an order authorizing your broker to buy a certain stock at a certain price lower than the market price. If the stock were to go lower, he wouldn't mind buying 100 shares. If the stock were to go higher he would keep the premium for not buying anything.

Double Leverage

The writer of a put with a long position in the stock must be very constructive towards the stock, since the position has double leverage (both on the upside and on the downside).

On the upside a profit will accrue from the stock going up, plus the premium from selling the put. However, when the stock declines, the value of the investor's position will drop twice as fast as the stock price.

Let's illustrate how a "short put, long stock" position would do either (1) when the underlying stock rises as anticipated, or (2) when the stock declines instead of rising as anticipated.

1. Upside Double Leverage

Double leverage on the upside will result if the underlying stock rises as anticipated.

Illustration:

On Sept. 2, 1977, Santa Fe International (SAF) traded at 46⅜ when its April 50 put was 5½:

Strike Price	Put Price	Stock Price
50	5½	46⅜

If an investor assumed the following "short put, long stock" position:

Long 100 shares of SAF at 46⅜

Short 1 SAF Apr 50 put at 5½

As of Nov. 25, 1977 SAF had risen to 53½ when its Apr 50 put had declined to 1⅞. The investor would benefit from the upside double leverage, including (1) a 7⅛-point profit accrued from the long stock position rising in price and (2) a 3⅝-point gain resulting from the short put position diminishing in value as follows:

87

	Long Stock	Short Put
9/2/77 Stock bought	46⅜	
9/2/77 Put sold		5½
11/25/77 Stock value	53½	
11/25/77 Put value		1⅞
Gain or (Loss)	7⅛	3⅝

2. *Downside Double Leverage*

Double leverage on the downside will occur if the underlying stock declined instead of rising as anticipated.

Illustration

On Sept. 2, 1977 Reserve Oil & Gas (RVO) traded at 17⅜ when its Feb 20 put was 3¼.

If an investor assumed the following "short put, long stock" position

Long 100 shares of RVO at 17⅜

Short 1 RVO Feb 20 put at 3¼

As of Nov. 25, 1977, RVO had declined to 14½ while its Feb 20 put had risen to 5¼. The investor would suffer from a downside double leverage from (1) a 2⅞-point loss on the "long stock" position and (2) a 2-point erosion on the "short put" position as follows:

	Long Stock	Short Put
9/2/77 Stock bought	17⅜	
9/2/77 Put sold		3¼
11/25/77 Stock value	14½	
11/25/77 Put value		5¼
Gain or (loss)	(2⅞)	(2)

Part IV

PUT SPREADING

Chapter 10

PUT SPREADING: WHY & HOW

What:
Put spreading is the simultaneous purchase and sale of puts of different series within the same class.

Why:
A spreading position is to reduce the risk inherent in a single long or short put position. However, the same action that reduces a spreader's risk also lowers his potential profit.

How:
Spreads between two options sometimes deviate from their normal patterns for short periods of time. Thus, a spreader may be able to capture such value or price discrepancy either due to temporary deviation from normal patterns, or from other market forces.

WHY & HOW

Put spreading is the simultaneous purchase and sale of puts of different series within the same class. The same types of spreads may be used with puts as with calls. Let's review the basic concept of spreading which applies to puts and calls alike.

Basic Concept
Spreading is essentially a hedging strategy. Its concept was borrowed from the commodity futures markets. Essentially, spreads are an application of the century-old arbitrage technique in the field of commodity options, utilizing the basic concepts of price differentials and time dissipation of premium.

The primary reason for entering into a spread position, is to reduce the risk inherent in a single long or short position. However, the same action that reduces a spreader's risk also lowers his potential profits. Thus, spreading is another form of a trade-off between risk reduction and profit-potential limitation characteristic of most option strategies.

"Dollar Difference"
Simply stated, spreading is the simultaneous purchase and sale of options on the same stock. A spread is the dollar difference between the buy and sell premiums. Its object is to capture the difference in premiums between the "long" option and the "short" option.

Illustration
On Nov. 11, 1977, Honeywell (HON) had the following Feb 45 and Feb 50 puts when the stock was 47¾:

Strike price	Feb	Stock price
45	1⅛	47¾
50	3⅜	47¾

You could buy HON Feb 50 put at 3⅜ and sell HON Feb 45 put at 1⅛ as follows:

Buy HON Feb 50 put at 3⅜
Sell HON Feb 45 put at 1⅛
Dollar Difference (Spread) 2¼

The spread (2¼) is the dollar difference between the buy and sell put-option premiums. An option is said to be "long" when you buy it; an option is said to be "short" when you sell it.

"Relative" Vs. "Absolute"
A spreader is less concerned with the high or low option premium levels than with the extent of spread between the premium' paid and the premium received in establishing the spread position.

When a particular put sells at an excessive premium, the other related puts will also usually sell at proportionately high premiums. These premiums will tend to balance each other.

By entering into a spread transaction rather than purchasing a put, we generally do not have to pay an extra amount when puts are selling at exceptionally high premiums. This enables the spreader to trade in the more volatile issues without paying high premiums.

"Simultaneous" Long and Short

Spreads are actually two separate option contracts in one transaction. While composed of two distinctly individual options, a spread option order cannot be executed unless both sides of the order are executed. This is because the two-orders-in-one is in fact entered as a unit order.

A whole array of spread techniques is available for sophisticated investors, depending on their view of market trends and of particular underlying stocks.

Despite their varying construction, all forms of spreading have at least one thing in common; that is, they contain "simultaneous" long and short positions on the same option with different strike prices and/or different expiration months.

Meaning Of "Debit" vs. "Credit"

The "spread" is expressed as a "debit" if the cost of the long put is *more* than the proceeds of the put sold.

Illustration

On Nov. 11, 1977, Avon (AVP) had the following July 45 and July 50 puts when the stock was 47⅜

Strike Price	Put Price	Stock Price
45	2⅛	47⅜
50	4¾	47⅜

If you bought AVP July 50 put at 4¾ and sold AVP July 45 put at 2⅛ you would have a "debit" of 2⅝ as follows:

Buy AVP July 50 put at 4¾

Sell AVP July 45 put at . . . .<u>2⅛</u>

Debit 2⅝

The "spread" is termed a "credit" if the cost of the long put is less than the proceeds of the put sold.

Illustration

On Nov. 11, 1977, General Motors (GM) had the following May 60 and May 70 puts when the stock was 67⅛.

Strike Price	Put Price	Stock Price
60	1⅞	67⅛
70	5½	67⅛

If you sold GM July 70 at 5½ and bought GM July 60 at 1⅞, you would have a "credit" of 3⅝ as follows:

Sell GM July 70 at 5½

Buy GM July 60 at 1⅞

Credit 3⅝

A spread is said to be "even" when the cost of buying an option is equal to that of selling an option.

SPREAD CONSTRUCTION

Varying Spread Combinations

Since normally there are three different expiration months and, in many cases, multiple strike prices, there is a great variety of spreading combinations typically available in many put classes.

In addition, different ratios of long to short may be devised to fit the individual investor's expectations and objectives. Different spreads involve different degrees of risk and are among the most complicated of option transactions.

Principal Spread Forms

The two principal forms of spread techniques are the price spread and the time spread.

1. Put Price Spread

Also called a "money" or "vertical" spread, a price spread is the purchase of a listed option and sale of a listed option having the same expiration month but a different strike.

In a put price spread, the two puts have different strike prices but the same expiration month.

94

Illustration

On Nov. 14, 1977, ABC Broadcasting (ABC) had the following May 40 and 45 puts when the stock was 42⅛:

Strike Price	May Put Price	Stock Price
40	2¼	42⅛
45	5	42⅛

You would establish a put "price" spread if you bought ABC 45/strike price put and sold 40/strike price put as follows:

Buy 45/strike price put at 5
Sell 40/strike price put at 2¼

Debit 2¾

2. *Put Time Spread*

Also called a "calendar" or "horizontal" spread, a time spread is the purchase of a listed option and the sale of a listed option having the same strike price but different expiration months.

In a put time spread, the two puts have different expirations but the same strike price.

Illustration

On Nov. 14, 1977 IBM had the following January and April puts with the strike price of 260 when the stock was 258¼

Strike Price	Jan	Apr	Stock Price
260	6½	9⅛	258¼

You would establish a put "time" spread if you bought Apr 260 at 9⅛ and sell Jan 260 at 6½ as follows:

Buy Apr 260 put at 9⅛
Sell Jan 260 put at 6½

Debit 2⅝

Value Deviation

Spreads between two options sometimes deviate from their normal patterns for short periods of time, especially when a new

strike price is added to the existing strike prices or when a new
expiration month is added to the current expiration months.

When new expiration months or strike-price options are first
available, there may be a preponderance of either buyers or
sellers, which unbalances the price of such options, while the
other outstanding options remain at their normal price levels.

The trader who is familiar with the spread pattern of a particular issue can profit from spreads that for short periods of time get
out of line from their normal patterns.

Potential Risk and Reward

Before an investor enters into a spread he should carefully read
and understand the Options Clearing Corporation's prospectus
and review his risk assumption as well as his potential reward
with his broker.

The appeal of option spreading has been greatly enhanced by
the adoption of margin rules that require a relatively small cash
outlay to enter into a position. After the initial spread is paid for,
no additional costs or additional margin is required as with certain
other spreading strategies. In the above IBM illustration, the cost
of spreading is limited to the "debit" of 2⅝ plus commissions.

It should be pointed out here, however, that although the risk
is known and limited, it could be considerable. Spreading transactions sometimes can produce losses of up to 100% of the amount
invested, although gains of up to 200% or more are possible.

Commission and Tax Factors

As a result of the high profit potential and definable risk involved, many investors have jumped into spreading without a full
awareness of all of the pitfalls.

First, commissions on spreads are high because each spread involves at least two option contracts, and they are more often than
not followed by a closing (liquidating) transaction before expiration. A closing transaction would then involve at least two additional option contracts. Thus the initiation of a spread and its subsequent liquidation would involve a minimum of four contracts.

The commissions involved might very well take away substantial, if not all of, the gains from spreading.

Second, an investor should consult his tax advisor prior to entering into spread positions because tax treatment of various possible results of a spread position may be advantageous or disadvantages.

PUT SPREAD MARGINS

General Put Margin Requirements

Spreads can be executed only in margin accounts. A position is considered a spread for margin purposes if both options are of the same class, and if the long option expires no earlier than the short option. A $2,000 minimum initial margin requirement applies to spreads. In addition, the long option must be paid for in full.

The margin required on a put spread position is the *lesser* of the following:

(A) The amount by which the strike price of the short put exceeds the strike price of the long put.

(B) The amount required to margin the short put, i.e., 30% of the margin value of the underlying security, *plus* the amount in-the-money, or *minus* the amount out-of-the-money, with $250 per contract minimum.

Put Margin Calculations

The following illustrations are designed for easier understanding of the above formulas for calculating put spread margins:

1. *Out-of-The-Money Margin Calculation*

   Illustration

   On Nov. 15, 1977 Northwest Industries (NWT) had the following June 45 and 50 puts when the stock was 53¼:

Strike Price	June Put Price	Stock Price
45	1	53¼
50	2½	53¼

Assume an investor sold a June 50 put for 2½ and bought a June 45 put for 1

```
Sell June 50 at ................................. 2½
Buy June 45 at .............................. 1
                                              ____
Credit ..................................... 1½
```

Margin is calculated below:
Under Rule (A):

```
Difference in strike prices (50−45) ............ $500.00
less Premium received ....................... 150.00
                                              _____
Margin ............................... $350.00
```

Under Rule (B):

30% of stock value ($5,324) $1,597.20
less Out-of-the-money amount of the short option
 ($5,324 − $5,000)......................   324.00
                                        $1,273.20
                                           150.00
         Margin $1,123.20

The lesser of the above two:
    $350.00 under Rule (A)
    $1,123.20 under Rule (B)
is $350.00 which would be required of this investor in
addition to the $150.00 premium received.

If, however, there were other securities or cash in his
account, the margin requirement would be $1,850.00
($2,000.00 less the $150.00 premium received).

The long put ($100) would, in any case, have to be
paid in full.

2. *In-The-Money Calculation*

On Nov. 15, 1977, General Motors (GM) had the following July 60 and 70 puts when the stock was 66⅝:

Strike Price	July Put Price	Stock Price
60	2	66⅝
70	6	66⅝

Assume an investor sold GM July 70 for 6 and bought
GM July 60 for 2:

Sell July 70 at 6
Buy July 50 at 2

    Credit 4

Margin is calculated as below:
Under Rule (A):
Difference in strike prices (70−60)...........$1,000.00
less Premium received 400.00

    Margin 600.00

Under Rule (B):
30% of stock value (66⅝) $1,998.75
plus In-the-money amount of the short option
    (70−66⅝) 337.50

    Margin $1,661.25

The *lesser* of the above two:
  $600.00 under Rule (A)
  $1,661.50 under Rule (B)
    is $600.00.

Chapter 11

PUT TIME SPREADS

What:
Also called "horizontal" or "calendar" put spread, a put time spread involves the purchase of a put and the sale of a put having the same strike price but different expiration months.

Why:
A spreader may gain in two ways. First, a spread will widen if the stock price approaches the strike price of the options. (A loss will result from a spread narrowing if the stock moves away, in either direction, from the strike price.

How:
Spreading will widen or narrow through the (1) passage of time and (2) movement in the price of the underlying stock.

The spread between two options tends to be the greatest when the stock is trading at the exercise price.

PRINCIPLE OF PUT TIME SPREADING

Different Expiration Months
As with call time spreads, put time spreads involve options of different expiration months but the same strike price. You can use time spreads either for bullish or bearish purposes.

In a bull put time spread, you sell (short) the further-out-month put and buy the closer-by-month put. Conversely, in a bear put time spread, you buy the further-out month put and sell (short) the closer-by put.

Time spreads provide a built-in protective advantage. The principal value of the time spread is that it gives the trader a degree of protection in the event that his judgment proves incorrect on the near term movement of the underlying stock.

This strategy is generally impractical for puts so far as the average investor is concerned because of premature exercise problem.

How To Widen The Spread

As with call time spreads, the theory of put time spreads is that, as time passes, the spreads will widen. As time passes, the distant spread will become the nearby spread.

Illustration

Assuming XYZ has the following puts with the strike price of 100 when the stock trades at 100:

	Feb.	May	Aug.	Stock Price
Strike Price 100	4	7	9	100

Note that the difference between the near (Feb) put and the middle (May) put is 3 (7−4) while the difference between the middle (May) put and the far (August) put is 2 (9−7).

Knowing that, with the passage of time as the further-out spread will become the nearby spread, and as the difference between the May and August premiums will widen, the investor might buy the August for 9 and sell the May for 7 to establish the following spread with a 2-point debit:

Buy Aug 100 put at 9
Sell May 100 put at . . . . <u>7</u>

Debit 2

If, at February expiration, XYZ remains at 100, the relationship between the May and the August premium might approximate the above relationship between the February and the May premium. Their spread might then widen to 3, and the spreader might liquidate his position at a 1-point profit, being the difference between the widened 3-point spread and the original 2-point spread as follows:

May put	Aug put	Credit (Debit)
Sold at 7	Bought at 9	(2)
Bought at 4	Sold at 7	3
Profit 3	(Loss) 2	1

In the above illustration of XYZ, assuming that the stock stands still at expiration, the spread will widen over time. If, however, instead of standing still, the stock could either go up or down. If it rose, say, to 110, both puts would narrow and the spreader would lose money. Also, if the stock declined, say to 90, both puts would be selling near their intrinsic value of 10. Again, the spread would narrow and the investor would lose money.

Two Key Factors

Let's examine a little more closely the potential impact of the two key factors: (1) time passage; and (2) stock price movement.

1. *Time Passage*

As time passes, assuming no movement in the price of the underlying stock, the spread tends to widen, that is, the spread between the two most distant expiration months will be less than that between the two nearby expiration months.

The ideal point to initiate a put time spread is just before the time value begins to diminish rapidly, which would be approximately 4 to 6 weeks before expiration. This would allow the spreader to take advantage of the drop in premium value while, at the same time, obtaining a further-out put which will lose its time value at a much slower pace.

2. *Stock-Price Movement*

The spread between two options tends to be the greatest when the underlying stock is trading at the exercise price. The spread between options tends to narrow as the underlying stock moves in either direction, away from the exercise price.

If the anticipated price movement in the underlying stock does not occur at expiration, the spread will suffer a loss. Therefore, it is important to have an opinion on the likely direction of the stock (bullish, bearish or neutral).

Two Ways To Profitability

A spreader may gain in two ways. First, a spread will widen if the stock price approaches the strike price of the options. (On the other hand, a loss will result from a spread narrowing if the stock moves away from the strike price in either direction.)

Second, the spread will also widen if the short put expires unexercised (or is repurchased for a small amount), leaving the long put held for a possible rise in value.

In our above illustrative spread on XYZ:

Buy Aug 100 put at 9
Sell May 100 put at 7

Debit 2

In the first instance, if the stock stands still at expiration, the spread will widen to 3, allowing the spreader to liquidate his position at a 1-point profit (3−2).

In the second instance, if the near (May) put expires worthless, the spreader will earn 7 (May put premium), thereby reducing the cost of his August put to 2 (9−7). He could realize a nice profit if the stock were to rise in value in the next three months. If not, the most he could lose would be the cost of the spread (2).

Generally, the movement in the price of the underlying security has a greater impact on the spread than does the passage of time.

Keys To Sound Spreading

Since successful time spreading depends upon a faster shrinking in the value of the short option than the long option, to be effective, time spreads generally require a short option with a large time value.

Also, a narrow spread premium differential is a prerequisite to sound time spreading. Spread differential is the difference between the premium you pay for the long position and what you receive for the short one.

In the above illustration of XYZ, the spread debit or differential is 2. All things being equal, one spread with a debit of 1½ would be more desirable than another spread with a debit of 2.

In entering a time spread order, it is important to obtain the best possible spread difference. Even a small fraction is vital because it usually accounts for a high percentage of the investment.

103

THREE PRINCIPAL APPROACHES

Bullish, Bearish Or Neutral

Put time spreads can be used when you are bullish or bearish, or when you expect the stock to remain flat or neutral. In other words, there are three principal approaches to put time spreading, namely:

1. Neutral approach—using at-the-money puts.
2. Bullish approach—using in-the-money puts.
3. Bearish approach—using out-of-the-money puts.

Neutral Approach—Using At-The-Money Puts

A neutral put time spread strategy using at-the-money put options is designed for investors who believe that a particular security will not move appreciably over the near term.

This strategy is based on the theory that as the far spread becomes the nearby spread with the passage of time, the difference between the premiums of the two options will widen.

Illustration

On Dec. 6, 1977, ABC Broadcasting (ABC) had the following near-the-money put options when the stock traded at 40:

	Feb.	May	Aug.	Stock Price
Strike Price 40	$1^{15}/_{16}$	2¾	2⅞	40⅛

A neutral put time spread might be set up with a ⅛-point debit as follows:

Buy Aug 40 at 2⅞
Sell May 40 at . . . .<u>2¾</u>

Debit . . . . ⅛

It's important to sell a large-value closer-by put (relative to the further-out put being bought) in order to make such a spread feasible.

If, at February expiration, ABC remained unchanged at 40, the relationship between the May put and the August put might approximate that between the February put and the May put. As indicated below, the spread might then be sold at a $^{11}/_{16}$-point profit.

	May Put	Aug Put	Credit/(Debit)
Sold	2¾	Bought 2⅞	(⅛)
Bought	1$^{15}/_{16}$	Sold 2¾	$^{13}/_{16}$
Profit	$^{13}/_{16}$	(⅛)	$^{11}/_{16}$

Bullish Approach—Using In-The-Money Puts

An investor bullish on a particular security over the near term might consider using in-the-money put options in a put time spread.

This strategy is based on the theory that the spread tends to widen as the stock price approaches the strike price of the options.

Illustration

On June 14, 1977, ABC Broadcasting (ABC) had the following in-the-money put options when the stock traded at 43½:

	Aug.	Nov.	Feb.	Stock Price
Strike Price 50	6½	7	7¼	43½

A bullish put time spread could be structured by buying ABC Feb 50 at 7¼ and selling ABC Nov 50 at 7, indicating a debit of ¼ as follows:

Buy Feb. 50 at 7¼
Sell Nov. 50 at 7

Debit .... ¼

If, by November expiration, the stock had risen from 43½ to 50, the Nov 50 put would expire worthless. Meanwhile, the Feb 50 put would reflect some time value and might be selling at around 2½. Thus, the spread would have widened, with a profit of 2¼ (before transaction costs) to the investor as follows:

105

	Nov. 50 put		Feb. 50 put		Credit/(Debit)
Sold	7	Bought	7¼		(¼)
Expired	0	Sold	2½		1¾
Profit	7	(Loss)	(4¾)		2¼

The premature exercise problem for in-the-money puts is far more serious than for in-the-money calls. It is not unusual to see distant in-the-money puts exercised; this rarely occurs with distant in-the-money calls.

Rolling A Bullish Put Time Spread

In the above illustration, the spreader might have set up a bullish put time spread by utilizing the near and middle (August-November) puts instead of the middle and far (November-February) puts as follows:

Buy Nov 50 at 7
Sell Aug 50 at 6½
Debit ....½

The above spread would be set up with a debit of ½.

If the stock had gone up from 43½ to 50 just prior to the August expiration, the following relative price structure might emerge:

	Aug	Nov	Feb	Stock Price
Strike Price 50	½	3	5	50

The August put could be repurchased for ½ at a 6-point profit as follows:

Short position: Aug 50.........................6½
Repurchased position: Aug 50 ....½

6

The spread could then be re-established by selling the November put at 3.

If the underlying stock remained unchanged at 50 through the November expiration, the November put would expire worthless. Reflecting its remaining time value, the February put might be selling at 3½. If the February put was then sold, the following would be the profit/loss picture:

106

Aug 50		Nov 50		Feb 50		Credit/(Debit)
Sold	6½			Bought	5	1½
Bought	½	Sold	3			2½
		Expired	0	Sold	3½	3½
Profit	6	Profit	3	Loss	(1½)	7½

Bearish Approach—Using Out-Of-The-Money Puts

If a trader anticipates the underlying stock to go down towards the expiration of the short put, he should initiate a put time spread using a strike price lower than the stock price. In contrast, as illustrated above, when a trader expects the underlying stock to rise toward the expiration of the short put, he would initiate a put time spread using a strike price higher than the strike price.

The following is an illustration on the bearish time spreading strategy utilizing out-of-the-money puts.

Illustration

Assuming that XYZ had the following out-of-the-money puts when the stock traded at 55:

	Aug.	Nov.	Feb.	Stock Price
Strike Price 50	2	4	5½	55

A bearish put time spread might be set up with a 1½-point debit as follows:

Buy Feb 50 put at 5½
Sell Nov 50 put at 4

Debit 1½

If the investor's market assessment had proved correct, and the stock declined to approximate the strike price of 50 at November expiration, the November 50 put would expire worthless, while the February 50 put might be trading at 7, creating the following profit/loss picture:

	Nov 50	Feb 50		Credit/(Debit)
Sold	4	Bought	5½	(1½)
Expired	0	Sold	7	7
Profit	4	Profit	1½	5½

In other words, with the passage of the time, and as the stock price declined to the strike price of the put option, the spread would widen from 1½ to 7 points, indicating a 5½-point profit on the spread transaction.

If the investor's market assessment had proved wrong, and the stock advanced to 60, the November option would still expire worthless, while the February option would be given some value because of its remaining time. While it's possible that the original 1½-point spread might remain essentially unchanged, the spread would probably not have widened to a point where a profit would occur for the spreader.

Bearish Put Time Spread vs. Bearish Call Time Spread

Bearish put time spreads generally are more frequently used than bearish call time spreads. There are two reasons. First, since bearish put time spreads typically are structured with out-of-the-money options, the chance of exercise is less than with bearish call time spreads, where in-the-money options would be utilized.

Second, an out-of-the-money put tends to have a larger time value than an in-the-money call. The key to profitable time spreading (whether call or put) depends, to a great extent, on the diminishing time value of the short option.

Note that all of our illustrations on put time spreads (bullish, bearish or neutral) involve buying the further-out options and selling the closer-by options. This is due to the infrequent use of put time spreads which involve selling the further-out options and buying the closer-by options. The reasons for the general reluctance to use the latter-type time spreads are two-fold. For one thing, they require much higher margin requirements. For another, the passage of time tends to work against such spreads.

Chapter 12

PUT PRICE SPREADS

What:

Also called "vertical" or "money" spread, a put price spread involves the purchase of or sale of a put having the same expiration month but different strike prices.

Why:

A price spread is set up with the expectation that the spread would narrow so that it would be bought back for less than it was originally sold.

How:

Like call price spreads, put price spreads can be used both for bullish and bearish purposes. In a bullish put price spread, you sell the higher strike price and buy the lower strike price. In a bearish put spread, you would do the reverse.

Vertical Structure

A put price spread consists of two puts which have the same expiration month but different strike prices shown in a *vertical* line in daily newspaper option-price tables. The following is an example of such a "vertical" listing on the June puts of Northwest Industries (NWT) with the strike prices of 50 and 55 on Nov. 14, 1977:

Strike Price	June	Stock Price
50	3	52
55	5	52

Since a price spread is composed of two options with different strike prices, and such strike prices are listed "vertically" in newspaper financial pages, such a spread is also called a "vertical" spread.

Like call price spreads, put price spreads can be used both for bullish and bearish purposes.

Essentially, a bull put spread is "long" the less expensive put and "short" the more expensive put. Conversely, a bear put spread is "long" the more expensive put and "short" the less expensive put. In other words, a bullish approach calls for selling a higher-strike-price put and buying a lower-strike-price put. A bearish approach involves buying a higher strike price put and selling a lower strike price put.

Call and put price spreaders differ in their attitude toward exercise. While a bull spreader in puts is hurt by exercise, a bull spreader in calls welcomes exercise. Conversely, while a bear spreader in puts welcomes exercise, a bear spreader in calls does not.

BULLISH APPROACH—SELL HIGHER STRIKE, BUY LOWER STRIKE

Risk In One-Sided Simple Buying

If an investor were bullish on a certain stock he might consider writing (selling) a put with the expectation that the stock would go up and the option premium would be retained. There is considerable risk in this one-sided simple selling, however. If the underlying stock should decline instead of rising as anticipated, he might have to buy the stock back at a price much higher than the original market price upon exercise of the option.

Risk-Reducing Element

To reduce the risk in this situation, the investor might also buy a put with a lower strike price.

Illustration

Assuming that XYZ had the following puts when the stock traded at 45:

Strike Price	Put Price	Stock Price
40	3	45
45	6	45

An investor who was bullish on XYZ and who only

wrote (sold) a put might select the at-the-money 45 put because its price would have the highest correlation with a move in the underlying stock. This simple-selling strategy would be based on the expectation that the underlying stock would go up, the 45 put would expire worthless, and the put premium of 6 would be retained. The seller's (writer's) maximum profit would be 6 (the premium received).

However, if the stock should fall from 45 to zero, which would be theoretically possible, there would be a risk of 39 per the calculation below:

Stock price	45
less Put premium received	6
Theoretical risk	39

To reduce the risk inherent in this situation, the investor might consider buying a lower-strike-price 40 put at 3 to establish the following bullish price spread:

Sell July 45 put at	6
Buy July 40 put at	3
Spread credit	3

The above spread would be set up with the expectation that the spread would narrow so that it would be bought back for less than it was originally sold.

Let's analyze the above spread from the viewpoint of potential profit versus potential risk.

On one side of the scale, the potential profit would now be limited to the spread credit of 3 (the difference between the sell premium of 6 and the buy premium of 3) instead of the premium of 6 received under the simple-selling strategy.

On the other side of the scale, the potential risk would now be limited to 2 per the calculation below:

Difference in strike prices (45−40)	5
less Spread credit received	3
Potential risk	2

The potential profit of 3 versus the potential risk of 2 would be considered an acceptable risk/reward ratio (explained in the sections below regarding how to calculate the maximum potential profit, the maximum potential risk and the spread break-even point).

The maximum profit for the spread would occur when the underlying stock at expiration went beyond the higher strike price of 45 which would render both puts worthless. The spread would have thus narrowed to zero, and the spreader would realize the maximum gain of 3 (6−3).

On the other hand, if the stock should fall below the lower strike price of 40 at expiration, the long 40 put would expire worthless, while the short 45 put would be selling at its intrinsic value of 5 (45−40). The spread would have widened to 5 points and the spreader would realize the maximum potential loss of 2 per the calculation below:

Short put value 5
less Spread credit originally received 3

2

HOW TO CALCULATE THE POTENTIAL SPREAD PROFIT/RISK

Calculation of Potential Spread Profit
In our previous illustration on XYZ, the maximum potential spread profit equals the spread credit (the differential between the sell and buy premiums):

Sell premium 6
Buy premium 3

Maximum potential profit 3

Calculation Of Potential Spread Risk
On the other hand, the maximum potential spread risk equals to the strike differential (the difference between the strike prices), *less* the spread credit.

In other words, the sum of the maximum potential profit and the maximum potential risk equals the strike differential (the dif-

112

ference between the strike prices). It follows that the *greater* the maximum potential spread profit, the *lesser* the maximum potential spread risk.

How To Maximize Spread Profit/Risk

Thus, in order to maximize the potential spread profit, experienced traders would not consider *selling* a price spread unless they can sell it at a credit of no less (preferably more) than 60% of the difference between the strike prices.

In our XYZ illustration, the spread credit of 3 equals to 60% of the strike differential of 5 and is, thus, in line with the above credit of no less than 60% of the spread selling guideline.

By the same token, experienced traders would not consider *buying* a price spread unless they can buy it at a debit of no more (preferably less) than 40% of the strike differential (the difference between the strike prices).

As opposed to *selling* a price spread (which is a bullish approach), *buying* a price spread is a bearish spread which will be discussed below.

Calculation Of The Spread Break-Even Point

The spread break-even point is the price at which the underlying stock may sell on the last option trading day and return your initial investment (potential spread risk). It is computed by adding the potential spread risk to the strike price of the long option.

5-Point Vs. 10-Point Spread Calculations

The above rules regarding (1) *selling* a spread at a credit of no less than 60% of the spread or (2) *buying* a spread at a debit of no more than 40% of the spread apply both to a 5-point spread and to a 10-point spread.

1. 5-Point Spread Calculations

In a 5-point spread, the maximum potential profit plus the maximum potential risk totals 5 points. In our above XYZ illustration, the maximum potential profit is 3, the maximum potential risk is 2 (5−3). If the maximum potential profit were 3½, the maximum potential risk would be 1½ (5−3½) per calculations below:

(A) Calculation Of Potential Profit

113

Assuming: Sell premium 4

     Buy premium .... ½

less Potential spread profit 3½

(B) Calculation Of Potential Risk
     Spread differential (45−40) 5
less Potential profit 3½

     Potential spread risk 1½

(C) Calculation Of Break-Even Point
     Strike price of the long option 40
plus Potential risk 1½

     Break-even point 41½

2. *10-Point Spread Calculations*
    In a 10-point spread, the maximum potential profit plus the maximum potential risk totals 10 point. In order to maximize the potential spread, experienced traders would not consider *selling* a price spread at a credit of less than 60% (or 6 points) of a 10-point spread, or *buying* a price spread at a debit of more than 40% (or 4 points) of a 10-point spread.

    Assuming the following XYZ 70-60 put price spread:
Sell XYZ 70 put at.............................9
Buy XYZ 60 put at 3

     Credit 6
The maximum profit, risk and break-even are calculated below:
(A) Calculation Of Potential Profit:
     Sell premium 9
less Buy premium 3
     Potential spread profit 6

(B) Calculation Of Potential Risk
     Spread differential (70−60) 10
less Potential profit 6

114

Potential spread risk 4
(C) Calculation of Break-even Point
Strike price of the long option 60
plus Potential risk 4
Break-even point 64

3. BEARISH APPROACH—BUY HIGHER STRIKE, SELL LOWER STRIKE

Instead Of Simple-Buying Strategy

If an investor were bearish on a certain stock, he might buy a put with the expectation that if the anticipated decline in the price of the underlying stock should take place, the value of the put would rise.

Assume XYZ had the following June puts when the stock traded at 50:

Strike Price	Put Price	Stock Price
45	3	50
50	5	50

The investor who was bearish on the stock, and who only bought a put, might select the at-the-money 50 put for 5 because its price would have the highest correlation with a move in the underlying stock. The risk of this simple-buying strategy would be limited to the purchase premium of 5, while its maximum profit potential would be 45, being the difference between the stock price of 50 and the purchase premium of 5, if the stock should decline to zero, which would be theoretically possible.

Risk/Reward Potential

To reduce his capital commitment as well as his maximum potential risk, the investor might consider *selling* a put with a lower strike price. In our above illustration, he might *sell* the 45 put for 3, thereby reducing his maximum risk from 5 to 2 (5−3):

Buy XYZ 50 put at 5
Sell XYZ 45 put at. 3

Debit. 2

In effect, he would be establishing a 50−45 bearish price spread at a debit of 2. While his maximum potential risk would now be limited to the initial 2-point debit, his maximum potential profit would now be limited to 3 per the calculation below:

Difference between the strike price (50−45) ..5

less Initial spread debit 2

Potential spread profit 3

The potential spread profit of 3 would amount to 60% of the 5-point spread and is thus in line with the spread-buying guideline's buying at a debit of no more than 40% of the spread.

How To Widen A Bear Put Price Spread

A bear put price spread should be structured with the purpose that it would widen to a point where it could be sold for more than what it had cost. This would occur if the anticipated decline in the price of the underlying stock should take place.

Illustration

Assume XYZ had the following August puts when the stock traded at 100:

Strike Price	Put Price	Stock Price
100	9	100
90	5	100
80	2	100

Further assume an investor initiated the following bear put price spread:

Buy Aug 100 put at 9

Sell Aug 90 put at 5

Debit 4

The above spread was set up at a 4-point (40% of the 10-point spread) with the expectation that the underlying stock would decline.

If the spreader's assessment should prove correct, and if the stock declined to the lower strike price of 90 or lower by August expiration, the August 90 put would expire worthless and the August 100 put would be selling at its intrinsic value of 10 points. The spread would widen to 10 as follows:

116

The long put (Aug 100) worth .10
The short put (Aug 90) worth . . . .<u>0</u>

                                                              10
The spreader would have a profit of 6 per calculation
below:
            Spread widened to 10
    less Spread originally bought at a debit of . . . .<u>4</u>

            Spread profit 6
    Thus, the spreader would have a 6-point profit, disre-
garding commissions.
    With the spread trading at any price below 90, the two
puts would rise in value point for point with the stock
decline.
    If the spreader's assessment of the underlying stock's
outlook were wrong, and if the stock did not decline
below 100 by August expiration, both puts would expire
worthless, and the spread would have narrowed to zero,
with a maximum loss of 4 points (the initial spread debit).

HOW TO ROLL A BEAR PUT PRICE SPREAD

    The bear put price spreader in our previous illustration might
consider rolling down to a new position if the spread should become profitable before August expiration:
Original Put Price Spread Structure
        The following was the original put price structure when
the stock traded at 100:

Strike Price	Put Price	Stock Price
100	9	100
90	5	100
80	2	100

with the following bear put price spread:
    Buy Aug 100 put at 9
    Sell Aug 90 put at . . . .<u>5</u>

        Debit 4

New Bear Put Price Structure

The following was the new bear put price spread structure when the stock declined from 100 to 90:

Strike Price	Put Price	Stock Price
100	10	95
90	4	94
80	2	95

If the spreader decided to liquidate his spread position, he could do so, since the spread had widened to 6 points (10−4) from the original 4-point spread.

The spreader might consider rolling down his position by buying the Aug 90 put for 4 in a closing transaction, and selling the Aug 80 put for 2 in an opening transaction. This would allow the in-the-money Aug 100 put to continue its upside profitability.

If the stock declined to 80 at the August expiration, the Aug 80 put would expire worthless, and the Aug 100 put would be selling at its intrinsic value of 20 (100−80).

The following is a table of the above rolling-down transactions:

Aug 100		Aug 90		Aug 80		Credit/(Debit)
Bought	9	Sold	5			(4)
		Bought	4	Sold	2	(2)
Sold	20			Expired	0	20
Profit	11	Profit	1	Profit	2	14

The above rolling transaction would result in a profit of 14 points. This would compare with the much smaller maximum profit potential of 6 points without the rolling operation.

There is considerable risk, however, in rolling a bearish put price spread. The primary risk is that the underlying stock might reverse its course and go back up, leading to the dissipation or even disappearance of the profit in the Aug 100 put. Should this occur, the relatively small profit remaining in the Aug 90 and Aug 80 puts would provide the only offsetting factor.

Part V

OTHER MULTIPLE OPTIONS

Chapter 13

STRADDLES

What:

A straddle is the purchase or sale of both a call and a put on the same underlying stock, with the same strike price, and the same expiration month.

Why:

Straddles provide both the buyer and the seller an opportunity to make money. Besides, they need not know the direction of the stocks on which they buy or sell straddles!

How:

For a straddle buyer to profit from his transaction, he needs only a sufficient fluctuation in the stock price, regardless of its direction. Straddle works best for buyers of volatile stocks due to the likelihood of fluctuation. The straddle seller would make money if the fluctuations in price remain narrow.

STRADDLE: Why And How

Most Common Combination

The advent of listed puts has made straddle an increasingly viable strategy. A straddle is the purchase or sale of both a call and a put on the same underlying stock, with the same strike price, and the same expiration date.

While calls and puts can be used together in various combinations, the straddle is probably the most common of such combinations.

121

Need Not Know Market Direction

Why have straddles developed into a major trading tool? Simply stated, straddles provide traders on both sides an opportunity to make money. Besides, they need not know the direction of the stocks on which they buy or sell straddles!

While call and put investors speculate on the market direction of a particular stock in a given time period, straddle investors need not know the direction of the market. For a straddle buyer to profit from his transaction, he need only a sufficient fluctuation in the price of the stock, regardless of its direction. Straddle works best for buyers of volatile stocks due to their likelihood of fluctuation. On the other hand, the *writer* who *sells* this straddle may also make a profit, if the fluctuations in price remain narrow.

Generally, a straddle buyer anticipates a substantial movement in the price of the underlying stock, but is uncertain as to the direction of that movement.

One would normally buy a straddle on a stock which has the potential to move far enough to make the straddle profitable within a specified period of time.

Illustration

On Nov. 8, 1977, ABC Broadcasting (ABC) had the following May 40 call and put when the stock was 39½:

	May 40	Stock Price
Call	2⅝	39½
Put	3	39½

If you expected ABC to have a significant move, you could buy a May 40 straddle, consisting of the following:

Buy ABC May 40 Call at 2⅝
Buy ABC May 40 Put at 3

Straddle cost 5⅝

How To Calculate Upper And Lower Profit Levels

To illustrate the method of calculating the upper and lower profit levels of a long straddle position, we use the ABC example:

Illustration

1. *Call Side*

The straddle would become profitable when the stock moved above 45⅝ per the following formula:

Strike price	40
Plus cost of straddle	5⅝
	45⅝

2. *Put Side*

The straddle would become profitable when the stock moved below 34⅜ per the following formula:

Strike price	40
Minus cost of straddle	5⅝
	34⅜

In other words, the straddle buyer would be profitable if the underlying stock rose above 45⅝ or declined below 34⅜.

On the other side of the trade, the profit or loss position for the straddle seller (writer) is just the opposite. He would become profitable if the stock stayed within the range of 34⅜–45⅝, which is appropriately called his zone of profitability.

In other words, a straddle seller (writer) would realize a profit as long as the price of the underlying stock remains within a narrow range, or more specifically, within a range of the exercise price plus or minus the total premiums involved.

General Ground Rules

As a rule, we advise the *sale* (*writing*) of straddles when it seems likely that the price of the stock will fluctuate within narrow bounds.

On the other hand, we advise the *purchase* of straddles if the price of the stock seems to show a definite trend. In this event, we expect one side of the straddle to produce a profit, while the other side provides insurance against a sudden and unexpected reversal of the trend.

As the market grows more volatile, straddle buying becomes

more attractive. This strategy is particularly attractive when option premiums are relatively low, since low premiums will mean a cheap straddle cost.

LONG STRADDLE

Importance of Volatility

The single most important rule for straddle buyers to remember is that the underlying stock will have to be volatile enough to make his straddle buying (or long straddle) position profitable.

A straddle buyer will be profitable if the stock moves far enough in *either* direction. In other words, he would profit from the *volatility* of the stock. His maximum risk is limited to the amount of his initial investment.

Other Key Criteria

In addition to volatility, straddle buyers should concentrate on those underlying stocks that most nearly fit the following key criteria:

1. Underlying stocks that sell at high price/earnings ratios.
2. Underlying stocks that sell for a high dollar price per share.
3. Underlying stocks that sell close to the high for the current year.

Which Expiration Month To Choose

In selecting the expiration month for buying straddles, we suggest the middle or far expiration months because their very length of time will permit the underlying stock to experience several substantial fluctuations in either direction during the life of the straddle.

The more frequent such fluctuations, the more trading opportunities presented to the straddle holder.

It should be pointed out, however, that the advantage inherent in a longer-maturity option is generally reflected in its price.

Basic Straddle Analysis

In order to help understand the straddle more fully, let's use the following basic illustration:

Illustration

Assume XYZ is at 50 when you establish a long straddle position by buying a 3-month call at 3 and a 3-month put at 2 as follows:

Buy XYZ 50 Call at	3
Buy XYZ 50 Put at	2
Straddle cost	5

If XYZ rose to 60, the straddle buyer would have a gain, from the call side, of $5 per share (or $500 per contract covering 100 shares) as follows:

50 Call's gain (60−50)	10
Straddle cost	5
	5

If XYZ rose further to 70, the straddle buyer would gain, from the call side, $15 per share (or $1,500 per contract), as follows:

50 Call's gain (70−50)	20
Straddle cost	5
	15

On the other hand, if XYZ declined from 50 to 40, the straddle still would have a gain of $5 per share, this time from the put side, as follows:

50 Put's gain (50−40)	10
Straddle cost	5
	5

If XYZ declined further to 30, the straddle would gain $15 per share also from the put side as follows:

50 Put's gain (50−30)	20
Straddle cost	5
	15

Only when the stock stood still or remained substantially unchanged would the straddle buyer suffer a loss because he would, in our example, lose $3 per share on the call side and $2 per share on the put side.

The following tabulates the profit and loss picture of the above straddle at expiration:

Stock Price at Expiration	Call Profit or Loss	Put Profit or Loss	Straddle Profit or Loss
30	−$ 300	+$1,800	+$1,500
40	−$ 300	+$ 800	+$ 500
50	−$ 300	+$ 200	−$ 500
60	+$ 700	−$ 200	+$ 500
70	+$1,700	−$ 200	+$1,500

Note that the straddle buyer will profit if the underlying stock moves far enough in *either* direction—up or down. He will incur a loss if XYZ stands still; however, his loss will be limited to his two option purchase premiums totaling $500. The maximum loss is pre-determined.

SHORT STRADDLE

Selling A Put and Call On The Same Stock, Same Strike, Same Expiration

A short straddle is a combination of one call and one put written on the same stock at the same strike price with the same expiration date.

Illustration

On Dec. 7, 1977, Honeywell (HON) had the following August 45 call and put when the stock traded at 45:

Strike Price	Call Price	Put Price	Stock Price
45	4⅝	3	45

A short straddle would be established if an investor sold both an Aug 45 call and an Aug 45 put as follows:

Sell Aug 45 call at 4⅝

Sell Aug 45 put at ....<u>3</u>

Total premiums 7⅝

The straddle was sold (written) with the expectation that the underlying stock would not move significantly either up or down.

Calculation Of Profit Parameters

The following is a simple method of calculating the profit parameters of a short straddle position:

1. *Straddle proceeds:*

   Call premium 4⅝

   Put premium 3

   Total proceeds 7⅝

2. *Upside Profit Parameter:*

   Strike price. 45

   plus Straddle proceeds 7⅝

   52⅝

3. *Downside Profit Parameter:*

   Strike Price 45

   less Straddle proceeds 7⅝

   37⅜

4. *Profitability Zone*

   52⅝ − 37⅜

You can figure out the potential profit zone of a straddle you are planning to sell (write) by simply using the straddle strike price plus or minus the total premiums you would receive for selling the straddle. The straddle seller will remain profitable so long as the underlying stock stays within a range of the exercise price *plus* (for the upside limit) or *minus* (for the downside limit) the total premiums received.

Even if the stock should move 4 points either up or down, the premiums received would still provide a sufficient cushion, resulting in an overall profit.

If the stock rose 4 points from 45 to 49, the call will be exercised at a 4-point loss (49−45) to the straddle writer, but the 7⅝-point total premiums received would more than cover the 4-point loss, resulting in an overall profit of 3⅝ (7⅝−4), disregarding commissions.

On the other hand, if the stock declines 4 points from

45 to 41, the put will also be exercised at a 4-point loss to the straddle seller. Here, too, however, the 7⅝ total premiums received still provide a gain of 3⅝ before commissions.

Risk of "Whipsaw"

Straddle sellers should be aware of the risk of major market moves in *either* direction. If the underlying stock *both* rises *and* declines during the life of the option, *both* the call *and* the put could be exercised, resulting in substantial losses.

If in our above illustration the stock initially drops 7 points from 45 to 38, the put might be exercised prior to expiration at a 7-point loss to the straddle writer. If subsequently the stock reverses its course and rises to 52, the call might also be exercised, resulting in a second 7-point loss to the straddle seller. The total loss of 14 points would only be partially offset by the 7⅝-point premium cushion, resulting in an overall loss of 6⅜ (14−7⅝) in our illustration.

Unhedged (uncovered) straddle sellers must always be aware of the possibility of "whipsaw" (a sharp price movement in one direction quickly followed by a sharp reversal in the opposite direction) and should at all times be prepared to *both* buy *and* sell the underlying stock at the option holder's discretion.

BULLISH VS. BEARISH APPROACH

An investor may buy or sell a straddle with a strike price *below* the stock price to give a bullish bias to the straddle position. On the other hand, he may buy or sell a straddle *above* the stock price to give a bearish bias to the straddle position.

A straddle position is considered bullish when it would need a relatively small up move for the straddle buyer to break even. On the other hand, a straddle position is considered bearish when it would require a relatively small down move for the straddle buyer to break even.

Generally an out-of-the-money put (with its strike price *below* the stock price) is used in structuring a bullish straddle.

Illustration

Assume XYZ had the following May calls and puts when the stock traded at 50:

Strike Price	Call Price	Put Price	Stock Price
May 45	6	2	50
May 50	3	4	50
May 60	1	11	50

Assume an investor established a bullish straddle buying position by using the May 45 call and put as follows:

Buy May 45 call at 6
Buy May 45 put at ....<u>2</u>

Straddle cost 8

(A) *Calculation Of Straddle Buyer's Position*

(a) The call side would become profitable at 53 per calculation below:

Strike price.............................45
plus Straddle cost ....<u>8</u>

53

(b) The put side would become profitable at 37 per calculation below:

Strike price.............................45
less Straddle cost ....<u>8</u>

37

(c) The straddle buyer would become profitable with the stock trading *above* 53 or *below* 37.

Since the underlying stock would have to make only a 2-point (4%) up move from 50 to 52 for the straddle buyer to break even, the straddle is considered a bullish one. On the other hand, the stock would have to decline 13 points (26%) from 50 to 37 before the straddle would break even.

(B) *Calculation Of Straddle Seller's Position*

The profitability zone for the straddle seller would

be just the reverse. The seller would become profitable with the stock trading between 37 and 53, and would lose money at any stock price either *above* or *below* that range.

Bearish Approach—Using In-The-Money Puts

Generally an in-the-money put (with a strike price *above* the stock price) is used in constructing a bearish straddle.

Illustration

Using the same put price data on the above XYZ illustration, an investor might establish a bearish straddle buying position by using the in-the-money May 60 call and put as follows:

Buy May 60 call at 1
Buy May 60 put at ....<u>11</u>

Straddle cost 12

(A) Calculation Of Straddle Buyer's Position

(a) The call side would become profitable at 72 per calculation below:

Strike price.............................60
plus Straddle cost ....<u>12</u>

72

(b) The put side would become profitable at 48 per calculation below:

Strike price.............................60
less Straddle cost ....<u>12</u>

48

(c) The straddle buyer would become profitable with the stock trading *above* 72 and *below* 48.

Since the underlying stock would have to make only a 2-point (4%) down move from 50 to 48 for the straddle buyer to break even, the straddle is considered a bearish one. On the other hand, the underlying stock would have to make a 12-point (24%) up move from 50 to 72 for the straddle to break even.

(B) Calculation Of Straddle Seller's Position

As compared with the straddle buyer's position, the straddle seller's would be just the reverse. He would be-

130

come profitable with the stock trading between 48 and 72, and would lose money at any stock price either *above* or *below* that range.

SHORT STRADDLE, LONG STOCK

With Or Without A Related Stock Position

The above discussion of short straddle assumes no long or short related stock exists at the time the straddle is sold (written). However, the sale of a straddle may be done with or without a long or short related stock position. The sale of a straddle obligates the seller to sell 100 shares of the underlying stock at the strike price.

A straddle seller with a long stock in the underlying stock is usually motivated by one of the following two beliefs. One is based on an extremely bullish view of the underlying stock, permitting the sale of a very expensive call. It is equivalent roughly to two covered writes. The other is based on the straddle seller's willingness either to sell his existing stock position at a higher price or buy additional stock at a lower price.

Many straddle sellers own the underlying stock as a means of generating premium income. Let's compare the risk-and-reward possibilities of the sale of a straddle alone with the combination of a straddle seller with a long position in the underlying stock.

Short Straddle Alone

Illustration

Assume the following May calls and puts on XYZ when the stock traded at 50:

Strike Price	Call Price	Put Price	Stock Price
May 45	6	2	50
May 50	3	4	50
May 60	1	11	50

Assume a straddle seller sold a May 50 call and a May 50 put:

Sell May 50 call 3
Sell May 50 put . . . .<u>4</u>

Straddle credit 7

He would make money between 57 and 43 per the calculation below:

1. *Upside Profit Level:*

Strike price 50

plus Straddle credit 7

_____

57

2. *Downside Profit Level:*

Strike price 50

less Straddle credit 7

_____

43

The following is a tabulation of profits and losses at various stock prices at expiration:

Profit or Loss

Stock Price	Call	Put	Premium Received	Profit or Loss
35	0	−15	7	−8
40	0	−10	7	−3
43	0	−7	7	0
45	0	−5	7	2
50	0	0	7	7
55	−5	0	7	2
57	−7	0	7	0
60	−10	0	7	−3
65	−15	0	7	−8

The maximum profit for the straddle seller would occur with the stock at expiration trading at the strike price of 50, which would render both the call and put written worthless, enabling the seller to retain the entire premium of 7 without further obligation.

As the stock at expiration moves away from the strike price either up or down, the straddle seller's profit would diminish. With the stock rising to 55 for instance, the call will be exercised by the holder at a 5-point loss to the straddle seller, but the premium received (7) would provide a cushion, resulting in an overall profit of 2 (7−5) to the straddle seller. The upside break even point exists at 57 when a 7-point loss on the call would be offset by the 7-point premium cushion.

If the stock declines to 45, the put will be exercised at a 5-point loss to the straddle seller; however, the 7-point premium cushion would again more than cover the call loss, with an overall gain of 2 (7−5) for the straddle seller. The downside breakeven point exists at 43, beyond which any further stock decline would result in an overall loss.

Combining Short Straddle With Long Stock

The inclusion of the stock makes the combination profitable at 46½ per the calculation below:

Strike price 50
Straddle premium:
  Call premium 3
  Put premium 4
less .... 7 ÷ 2 = 3½
                               46½

The maximum profit of 7 would be realized at any price above the strike price of 50 as indicated by the following tabulation showing the profit or loss results with the stock, at expiration, at different price levels:

Stock Price Levels Or (Loss)	Profit or (Loss) Call	Put	Premiums Received	Stock Profit or (Loss)	Total Profit Or (Loss)
35	0	−15	7	−15	−27
40	0	−10	7	−10	−13
45	0	−5	7	−5	− 3
46½	0	−3½	7	−3½	0
50	0	0	7	0	7
55	− 5	0	7	0	7
60	−10	0	7	10	7
65	−15	0	7	15	7

The breakeven point for this position occurs at 46½ when the 3½ point loss *each* on the short put and the long stock would be just offset by the 7-point premium cushion.

On the downside, this short straddle-long stock combination would lose money twice as fast as the sale of the straddle alone, because both the short put and the long stock would be moving against this investor.

How To Reduce The Risk In A Short Straddle

The following is an illustration of how to reduce the risk in a short straddle through the purchase of a call at a higher strike price and of a put at a lower strike price.

Illustration

On Dec. 12, 1977, Mesa Petroleum (MSA) had the following May calls and puts when the stock traded at 40:

Strike Price	Call Price	Put Price	Stock Price
35		1¼	40
40	4½	2⅞	40
45	2 5/16		40

1. Short Straddle Alone

Assume an investor sells a MSA 40 straddle alone:

Sell May 40 call at 4½
Sell May 40 put at 2⅞

Credit 7⅜

Such a short straddle with a 7⅜-point credit would be profitable between the following two parameters:

(A) Upside Profit Level:

Call strike price 40
plus Straddle credit 7⅜

47⅜

(B) Downside Profit Level:

Put strike price 40
less Straddle credit 7⅜

32⅝

Thus, the straddle would be profitable between 47⅜ and 32⅝.

134

However, the disadvantage of a short straddle alone is the potentially unlimited loss on the call if the underlying stock rises, and a virtually unlimited potential loss on the put if the stock falls.

2. *Short Straddle, Long Call, Long Put*

To limit the risk in a short straddle, an investor could buy a call at a higher strike price and a put at a lower strike price than the straddle strike price, as follows:

Buy May 45 call at ....2 $5/16$
Sell May 40 call at 4½
Sell May 40 put at 2⅞
Buy May 35 put at 1¼

Credit ....3$9/16$

Sell premiums of 7⅜ (4½+2⅞), *less* buy premiums of 3 $9/16$ (2$5/16$+1¼), result in an overall credit of 3$9/16$ for the entire position.

The addition of the out-of-the-money put and the out-of-the-money call has limited the potential loss, regardless of how far up or down the stock might move. In return for limiting the risk, the investor has paid two additional commissions and narrowed his profit range.

HOW TO CALCULATE STRADDLE MARGINS

Margin On A Long Straddle

A long straddle involves a long call and a long put. Both options must be paid for in full, and neither will have loan value in a margin account.

Illustration

On Dec. 12, 1977, Mesa Petroleum (MSA) had the following July 40 call and put when the stock traded at 40:

Strike Price	Call Price	Put Price	Stock Price
40	4½	2⅞	40

If you had no cash or other securities in your cash or margin account, and if you bought a July 40 call and a

July 40 put, you would have to deposit $738 per the calculation below as full payment for the call and the put:

Buy July 40 call (4½ × 100 shares) . . . . $450.
Buy July 40 put (2⅞ × 100 shares) $288

Total payment required $738

Margin On A Short Straddle

A short straddle involves a short call and a short put. The required margin will be the uncovered short requirement on the call or the put, whichever is *greater*.

Illustration

On Dec. 12, 1977, Northwest Industries (NWT) had the following March 55 call and put when the stock traded at 55½:

Strike Price	Call Price	Put Price	Stock Price
55	3	$2^{13}/16$	55½

If you had no cash or securities in your cash or margin account, and if you bought a March 55 call at 3 and a March 55 put at $2^{13}/16$, the required margin would be the *greater* of the following two computations:

(A) *Call Computation*

30% of stock price (55½) $1,665
plus Call in-the-money amount (55½−55) 50
Margin requirement $1,715
Premium received (3+2 13/16) 581

Margin call $1,134

(B) *Put Computation*

30% of stock price (55½) $1,665
less Put-out-of-the-money amount
(55½−55) 50

Margin requirement $1,615
less Put-out-of-the-money amount
(3+2 13/16) 581

Margin call $1,034

The *greater* of the above two computations is $1,134—the margin call which must be required.

Chapter 14

COMBINATIONS

What:
A combination is either the purchase or the sale of both puts and calls on the same underlying stock that have different strike prices and the same, or different expiration months.

Why:
Combination strategy offers the potential of increased leverage to the buyer and additional income to the seller.

How:
For a combination buyer to become profitable, it would require a substantial move in the underlying stock. While the buyer should look for volatile stocks to give him a greater chance for large stock movement, the seller should seek the opposite—stocks known for their lack of volatility.

In addition to straddles, there are other combinations of puts and calls that may be used effectively to accomplish various investment objectives.

Objectives of Combinations
A combination is either the purchase or the sale of both puts and calls (on the same underlying stock) that have different strike prices and the same, or different, expiration months. The combination strategy offers the potential of increased leverage to the buyer and additional income to the seller (writer).

The most important factor in the success of any of these combinations is the selection of the underlying stock. In order to be right in any combination option strategy, the investor should be dealing with the right stock.

Importance of Volatility
Of primary importance is volatility. Often a substantial move in

the underlying stock is required for a particular combination to become profitable.

Some knowledge of the degree of volatility in a particular stock provides the key to whether or not you should enter into any option combination strategy.

Should the buyer and the seller of combination options look for the same characteristics in selecting a combination? Definitely not! While the buyer should look for volatile stocks, the seller should seek the opposite—stocks known for lack of volatility. The seller would want a fairly neutral situation, a static stock expected to show little or no movement in either direction.

It would be equally important to the buyer or the seller of combination options to examine the price behavior of the underlying stock to see if, based on past price history it is capable of substantial moves. Like the buyer, the seller should weigh positions to conform with a judgment on market direction in general, and the direction of the underlying stock in particular. Most major brokerage houses have compiled a record of volatility for the most commonly held and most frequently traded stocks.

Margin requirements must be considered when evaluating the potential return on any combination position. Commission costs will also alter the figures somewhat.

Broad Vs. Narrow Meaning

In a broad sense, a combination option is anything that is not covered by the terms put, call, spread or straddle as currently defined on the listed option exchanges. The word "combination option" came into existence because the word "spread", as used in the over-the-counter option market, has taken on a new meaning in the listed option market. The most common "combination option" is probably what in the past was referred to as a spread, i.e., an option transaction where traders buy, or sell, one call and one put on the same underlying stock with either different strike prices, and/or different expiration months.

In the over-the-counter option markets, in addition to spreads, there are other forms of multiple options, including "strips" and "straps". A strip involves one call and two puts. On the other hand, a strap involves one put and two calls. Strips and straps account for a very small percentage of the over-the-counter option market. They have continued, and will probably continue to do so in the listed option market.

COMBINATION BUYING

Combination on The Same Expiration Month
This strategy involves the simultaneous purchase of a put and a call. Each of the options would have a different strike price.

For example, if the underlying stock is 50 and the stock has 45, 50 and 55 options, the combination buyer would purchase a 55 call and a 45 put. The purpose of combination buying is to trade one side against the other. Generally, the cash outlay should be small.

Long Call, Long Put (With Different Strike Prices)
The following is an actual illustration on combination buying of a put and a call that have different strike prices but the same expiration month.

Illustration
On Nov. 17, 1977, Santa Fe International (SAF) had the following April calls and puts when the stock was 50:

1. Calls

Strike Price	April Call Price	Stock Price
45	6⅞	50
50	3¾	50
55	1¾	50

2. Puts

Strike Price	April Put Price	Stock Price
45	$1^5/_{16}$	50
50	3⅜	50
55	6¾	50

Assume an investor bought an Apr 55 call at 1¾ and an Apr 45 put at 1 5/16:

Buy Apr 55 call at 1¾
Buy Apr 45 put at . . . .$1^5/_{16}$

Total cost . . . .$3^1/_{16}$

139

Since both the call and the put are out-of-the-money, the investor would require a relatively small cash outlay of $3^1/_{16}$. The total risk never could be more than the total cost of $3^1/_{16}$ for the combination buying position.

If the underlying stock moved enough to make position profitable, the leverage factor could be dramatic. At expiration, the combination buyer would make money if the stock were either above or below $41^{15}/_{16}$ per the calculation below:

Method of Calculation

1. The call side would become profitable if the stock rose above the call strike price *plus* the cost of the two options:

Call strike price 55
Plus cost of the two options . . . .$3^1/_{16}$

$58^1/_{16}$

The call would have intrinsic value with the stock above the call strike price of 55, in addition to overcoming the cost of the two options.

2. The put side would become profitable if the stock fell below the put strike price minus the cost of the two options:

Put strike price 45
Minus cost of the two options . . . . $3^1/_{16}$

$41^{15}/_{16}$

The put would become valuable when the stock declined below the put strike price of 45, in addition to overcoming the cost of the two options.

Maximum risk of $3^1/_{16}$ would occur at any stock price between $41^{15}/_{16}$ and $58^1/_{16}$.

The potential for movement in the underlying stock is all important when buying a combination. Volatility is the key word here.

Even though the actual dollars involved are relatively small, a 16% move on the upside (from 50 to above 58 $1/_{16}$) and a 16% move on the downside (from 50 to below

$41^{15}/_{16}$) would be necessary for this combination position to become profitable. The need for volatility is obvious.

Naturally, large sudden moves in the underlying stock prior to expiration also can provide momentary profits in the option even though the parameters ($58^{1}/_{16}$ and $41^{15}/_{16}$) were not breached.

It also follows that the longer the option time period, the more opportunity for changes in the price of the underlying stock. However, the longer-term option will invariably cost more, and this must be weighed against the potential for increased profits.

Combination options are normally done with both sides out-of-the-money. There are occasional instances, however, where either or both sides may be in-the-money.

Step-By-Step Procedure

The following illustration will examine in detail the step-by-step combination-buying procedure.

Illustration

On Nov. 18, 1977, Revlon (REV) had the following June call and put when the stock traded at 43

	Strike price	Option price	Stock price
Call	45 (out-of-the-money)	2	43
Put	40 (out-of-the-money)	$2\frac{1}{8}$	43

Notice that both the call and the put were out-of-the-money.

Assuming the following initial combination position:

Buy 1 June 45 call (2 × 100 shares) $200.00
Buy 1 June 40 put ($2\frac{1}{8}$ × 100 shares). $212.50

Total cost and risk $412.50

What you are shooting for is a sharp stock price movement in either direction. A sharp up move should cause a rise in the value of the purchased call while a large down move w,ill increase the value of the purchased put.

Tabulated below is where the call and the put would approximately trade at expiration date, based on various stock price levels:

Stock Price	June 45 Call	June 40 Put	Combination Cost	+ Profit − Loss
28 0		$+1,200	$412.50	$+787.50
31 0		+ 900	412.50	+484.50
34 0		+ 600	412.50	+187.50
37 0		+ 300	412.50	−112.50
40 0		0	412.50	−412.50
45 0		0	412.50	−412.50
48 .$+ 300		0	412.50	−112.50
51 . + 600		0	412.50	+187.50
54 . + 900		0	412.50	+484.50
57 . +1,200		0	412.50	+787.50

We summarize the above tabulation into the following "value at expiration" (no point):

	Put	Value	Zone		No	Value	Call	Value	Zone
Option Value	..12	.. 9	.. 6	.. 3	.. 0	.. 0	.. 3	.. 6	.. 9	..12
Stock Value	..28	..31	..34	..37	..40	..45	..48	..51	..54	..57

Two Basic Approaches

Once a combination buying position is established, there are two basic approaches to take. One would be to "lift a leg" (either call or put) to generate enough profit to cover the cost of the combination, and hold the other "free" leg to wait for an opportune time. The other approach would be to stay with both legs to wait for a major stock move.

1. *"Leg Lifting" Approach*

If either the call or the put side becomes sufficiently profitable to recoup the entire cost of the combination, liquidate the profitable side by a transaction known as "lifting a leg". The investor would hold the remaining option at virtually no cost in expectation that a decent profit will result.

Illustration

On July 28, 1977, Honeywell (HON) had the following Feb 60 call and Feb 50 put when the stock traded at 51⅛:

	Strike Price	Option Price	Stock Price
Call	60	1¼	51⅛
Put	50	2½	51⅛

Assuming an investor bought the following combination:

Buy Feb 60 call at 1¼
Buy Feb 50 put at 2½

Total Cost 3¾

As of Nov. 8, 1977, HON had declined to 45½ when its Feb 50 put had risen to 4⅞, which was more than the entire cost of the combination originally bought at 3¾. If the investor liquidated his Feb 50 put at 4⅞ by lifting the "put" leg, which would result in a 1⅛-point profit (4⅞−3¾), disregarding commissions, the remaining option (Feb 60 call) would be held at no cost to him, and could rise in value if the stock should subsequently recover.

2. *Aiming-At-High Approach*

The alternative approach would be for the investor to stay with both sides of the combination, hoping for a major move (up or down) in the price of the underlying stock.

Bullish Vs. Bearish Approach

To explain the bullish versus the bearish approach in combination buying, let's again use the Santa Fe International (SAF) and its April option price data as of Nov 17, 1977:

Strike Price	Call Price	Put Price	Stock Price
45	6⅞	$1^5/_{16}$	50
50	3¾	3⅜	50
55	1¾	6¾	50

1. *Original Position*

Assuming the following original combination-buying position:

Buy 55 Call at. 1¾
Buy 45 put at. . . . . $1^5/_{16}$

Total cost . . . . $3^1/_{16}$

143

(A) Call profit level:

Call strike price 55

plus Combination cost . . . . $3^1/_{16}$

Above . . . . $58^1/_{16}$

(B) Put profit level:

Put strike price 45

less Combination cost . . . . $3^1/_{16}$

Below . . . . $41^{15}/_{16}$

2. *Bullish Approach*

If an investor were somewhat partial to an up move in the stock, the original combination-buying position could be tilted upward in various ways. One way would call for buying a call with the strike price near the stock price, while buying the same put as follows:

Buy 50 call at . . . .

Buy 45 put at . . . . $1^5/_{16}$

Total cost . . . . $5^1/_{16}$

(A) Call profit level:

Call strike price 50

plus Combination cost . . . . $5^1/_{16}$

Above . . . . $55^1/_{16}$

(B) Put profit level:

Put strike price 45

less Combination cost . . . . $5^1/_{16}$

Below . . . . $39^{15}/_{16}$

3. *Bearish Approach*

If, on the other hand, an investor were partial to a down move in the stock, he could buy a put with the strike price near the stock price, and use the original call strike price at 55:

Buy 55 call at 1¾

Buy 50 put at 3⅜

Total cost 5⅛

(A) Call profit level:

Call strike price 55

plus Combination cost 5⅛

Above 60⅛

(B) Put profit level:

Put strike price 50

less Combination cost 5⅛

Below 44⅞

To summarize the above:
1. Original position:
   (A) Call profit above . . . . 58$^{1}/_{16}$
   (B) Put profit below . . . . 41$^{15}/_{16}$
2. Bullish Approach:
   (A) Call profit above . . . . 55$^{1}/_{16}$
   (B) Put profit below . . . . 39$^{15}/_{16}$
3. Bearish approach:
   (A) Call profit above 60⅛
   (B) Put profit below 44⅞

With Or Without Underlying Stock Position

The combination buyer may or may not have a related underlying stock position. Or he may be short the underlying stock.

1. Combination Buyer Without Stock Position

The buyer of a combination option without a position in the underlying stock generally holds the view that the stock is likely to make a major move on either the upside or the downside, or both. Like the straddle buyer, the combination buyer either takes the posture that the anticipated move in the underlying stock will be more than enough to cover the cost of the premiums paid for the two options, or utilizes the combination position as a trading umbrella.

2. Combination Buyer With Stock Position

For a combination buyer who owns the underlying stock, he considers the long put as "insurance" for the long stock position on the downside and the long call as added leverage on the upside.

145

3. *Combination Buyer With A Short Stock Position*

The combination buyer may be short the underlying stock and consider the long call as "insurance" on the upside and the long put as added leverage on the downside.

Variable Ratio Combination Buying

Instead of buying one call and one put, an investor could orient his position in the desired direction by varying the purchasing ratio (adding calls or puts).

A bullish investor may buy two calls and one put. Conversely, a bearish investor may buy two puts and one call.

Illustration

On Nov. 25, 1977, Eastman Kodak (EK) had the following July call and put when EK traded at 53:

	Strike Price	Option Price	Stock Price
Call	60 (out-of-the-money)	2⅜	53
Put	50 (out-of-the-money)	2½	53

Let's compare the following three:
1. One call to one put combination buying;
2. Two calls to one put combination buying; and
3. Two puts to one call combination buying.

1. One Call to One Put Combination Buying

Buy one 60 call at 2⅜

Buy one 50 put at 2½

Total cost 4⅞

(A) The call side would become profitable when the stock rose above 64⅞:

Call strike price 60

plus Combination cost 4⅞

64⅞

(B) The put side would become profitable when the stock fell below 45⅛:

Put strike price 50

less Combination cost 4⅞

45⅛

2. *Two Calls To One Put Combination Buying*

      Buy two 60 calls (2 × 2⅜) 4¾

      Buy one 50 put 2½

      Total cost 7¼

      (A) The call side would become profitable when the stock rose above 63⅝:

      Call strike price 60

plus Combination cost ÷ 2 . . . . .3⅝

                          63⅝

because the combination cost of 7¼ would allow profitability above 63⅝ (two calls at 60, plus 3⅝ each). For each 1-point move above 63⅝, the investor makes 2 points.

      (B) The put side would become profitable when the stock fell below 42¾:

      Put strike price 50

less Combination cost 7¼

                          42¾

3. *Two Puts To One Call Combination Buying*

      Buy two 50 puts (2 × 2½) at 5

      Buy one 60 call at 2⅜

      Total cost 7⅜

      (A) The call side would become profitable when the stock rose above 67⅜:

      Call strike price 60

plus Combination cost 7⅜

                          67⅜

      (B) The put side would become profitable when the stock fell below 46⁵/₁₆.

      Put strike price 50

less Combination cost ÷ 2 . . . . $3^{11}/_{16}$

                          46⁵/₁₆

because the combination cost of 3 11/16 would allow a profit on the puts below 46⅝ (two puts at 50, less $3^{11}/_{16}$ each).

To summarize the above:
   1. One call to one put buying:
      (A) Call profit above 64⅞
      (B) Put profit below 45⅛
   2. Two calls to one put buying:
      (A) Call profit above 67¼
      (B) Put profit below 42¾
   3. Two puts to one call buying:
      (A) Call profit above 67⅜
      (B) Put profit below 42⅝

COMBINATION SELLING

Short Call, Short Put (With Different Strike Prices)
The seller of a combination option is agreeing to both buy and sell 100 shares of the underlying stock at the respective strike prices. He is, in effect, selling a straddle, where the call and the put have different strike prices, primarily with the same expiration month.

Seeking A Static Stock
In selecting a combination, the seller should look for exactly the opposite to what the buyer would be seeking. As opposed to the buyer who would want a volatile stock, the seller would want a fairly neutral or static stock that is expected to show little movement in either direction. The underlying stock being volatile or static is generally reflected in its option premium.

The objective for a combination seller is income or cash flow. He takes in option money when a combination writing position is initiated. This money constitutes the maximum profit that may be obtained, provided that all options written expire worthless.

With Or Without Related Stock Position
The seller of a combination option may do so with or without a related stock position. A combination seller *without* a related stock position is said to be an uncovered combination seller. A combination seller *with* a related stock position is said to be a covered combination seller.

Uncovered Combination Seller
A combination seller with no position in the underlying stock

148

believes that the stock will remain static, or move so little that both options will expire worthless. Since an uncovered combination seller does not own the underlying stock and is naked, it would be desirable for him to write relatively shorter-term options in order to minimize the potential for fluctuation in the underlying stock.

Illustration

On Nov. 17, 1977, Santa Fe International (SAF) had the following April calls and puts when the stock was 50:

1. Call

Strike Price	April Call Price	Stock Price
45	6⅞	50
50	3¾	50
55	1¾	50

2. Puts

Strike Price	April Put Price	Stock Price
45	1 5/16	50
50	3⅜	50
55	6¾	50

Assume an investor sold an Apr 55 call at 1¾ and an Apr 45 put at $1^5/_{16}$ as follows:

Sell Apr 55 call at 1¾
Sell Apr 45 put at .... $1^5/_{16}$

Total income .... $3^1/_{16}$

The total income provided by selling the two options would total $3^1/_{16}$.

These options would expire worthless if the underlying stock stayed within the 16⅛-point range ($58^1/_{16}-41^{15}/_{16}$), per the calculation below:

1. Upper Profit Level:
    Call strike price 55
    plus Option income .... $3^1/_{16}$

                       $58^1/_{16}$

2. Lower Profit Level:
    Put strike price........................45
    minus Option income .... $3^1/_{16}$

                       $41^{15}/_{16}$

This 16⅛-point range is called the profit or safety zone for the seller. If the stock should rise above 58 $^1/_{16}$ or fall below 41$^{15}/_{16}$, the seller must close the position out. Exercises must be avoided, because they would create commission expenses on the underlying stock. Any closing that would cost more than the option money of 3$^1/_{16}$ received would result in a loss.

Unexpected events may cause large moves in the underlying stock, and the risk can be point for point beyond the profit or safety zone. Thus, the seller must pay even greater attention to the position than the buyer.

Like the combination buyer, the seller must weigh positions to conform with a judgment on market direction. As a result, the profit or safety range may be altered.

The above combination writing position on Santa Fe International (SAF), based on the Nov. 17, 1977 price data, can be altered by using either a call or a put that is closer to being in-the-money.

Nov. 17, 1977 SAF price data:

Strike Price	Call Price	Put Price	Stock Price
45	6⅞	1$^5/_{16}$	50
50	3¾	3⅜	50
55	1¾	6¾	50

1. Bullish Approach—Using A Put Closer To Being In The-Money

If the put is closer to being in-the-money than the call the combination seller's position would work better if the stock should rise.

Illustration

Thus, if instead of selling the 45 put for 1$^5/_{16}$, the seller had sold the 50 put for 3⅜, the combination would have been sold for 5⅛-point premiums per the calculation below:

Sell Apr 55 call at 1¾
Sell Apr 50 put at 3⅜

Total income 5⅛

The profit zone for the combination seller would be between the following two parameters:

(A) Upside Profit Level:

Call strike price 55
plus Premium income . . . . <u>5⅛</u>

60⅛

(B) Downside Profit level:
Put strike price 50
less Premium income . . . . <u>5⅛</u>

44⅞

(C) Profit Range:
Between 60⅛ and 44⅞

2. Bearish Approach—Using A Call Closer To Being An In-The-Money
Illustration

If, instead of selling the 55 call for 1¾, the investor had sold the 50 call for 3¾, the combination would have been sold with $5^{1}/_{16}$-point premiums per the calculation below:

Sell Apr 50 call at 3¾
Sell Apr 45 put at . . . . <u>$1^{5}/_{16}$</u>

Total income . . . . $5^{1}/_{16}$

The profit zone for the combination writer would be between the following two parameters:

(A) Upside Profit Level:
Call strike price at 50
plus Premium income at . . . . <u>$5^{1}/_{16}$</u>

$55^{1}/_{16}$

(B) Downside Profit Level:
Put strike price at 45
less Premium income . . . . <u>$5^{1}/_{16}$</u>

$39^{15}{}_{16}$

(C) Profit Range:
Between $55^{1}/_{16}$ and $39^{15}/_{16}$

To summarize the above, we would have the following different profit ranges:
(A) Original profit zone:

$$58^{1}/_{16} - 41^{15}/_{16}$$

(B) Bullish approach (with the put closer to being in-the-money):

$$60\frac{1}{8} - 44\frac{7}{8}$$

(C) Bearish approach (with the call closer to being in-the-money):

$$55\frac{1}{16} - 39\frac{15}{16}$$

Covered Combination Seller

A combination seller with a related long position in the underlying stock generally will be willing to sell his long position at the strike price of the call plus the two premiums received, or add to his existing position through the exercise of the put, should the stock decline.

Combination Seller With Short Stock Position

A combination seller with a short position in the underlying stock generally will be willing to let his short be covered by the exercise of the put plus the premium, should the stock depreciate, and is willing to be short additional shares should the underlying stock appreciate in price.

Varied Ratio Approach

Like the combination buyer, the combination seller may, depending on his view of the underlying stock, fine tune his position in the desired direction by adding puts or calls.

Illustration

Based on the Nov 17, 1977 April option price data on SAF:

Strike Price	Call price	Put Price	Stock Price
45	$6\frac{7}{8}$	$1\frac{5}{16}$	50
50	$3\frac{3}{4}$	$3\frac{3}{8}$	50
55	$1\frac{3}{4}$	$6\frac{3}{4}$	50

Instead of selling the following one-to-one combination:

Sell 1 Apr 55 call at . . . .$1\frac{3}{4}$

Sell 1 Apr 45 put at . . . . $\underline{1\frac{5}{16}}$

Credit . . . . $3\frac{1}{16}$

If the combination seller were bullish, he could sell two April 55 calls and only one Apr 45 put as follows:

152

Sell 2 Apr 55 calls @ 1¾ at 3½
Sell 1 Apr 45 put 1⁵/₁₆

Credit 4¹³/₁₆
The credit of 4¹³/₁₆ would allow the straddle seller to remain profitable between the following two parameters:
1. *Upside Profit Level:*
    Call strike price at. 55
plus Credit: 4¹³/₁₆ divided by 2 =   2¹³/₃₂

57¹³/₃₂
2. *Downside Profit Level:*
    Put strike price 45
less Credit . . . .·. 4¹³/₁₆

40¹³/₁₆
The above profit range of 57 13/32−40 13/16 for two call-and-one put combination selling compares with the profit range of 58 1/16−41 15/16 for one call-and-one put combination selling illustrated above.

Evaluating Each Component
Combinations offer infinite possibilities to enable investors to meet various goals.

Just remember to evaluate each component of the combination for its risks, as well as for its potential reward.

COMBINATION VERSUS STRADDLE

Relative Dollar Risks
A combination usually involves a put and a call of different strike prices which are both out of the money as follows, based on the previous Nov 17, 1977 SAF price data:
    Apr 55 call. 1¾
    Apr 45 put 1⁵/₁₆

Total premium 3¹/₁₆
Since, with the stock trading at 50, both Apr 55 call and Apr 45 put were out-of-the-money, their combination would cost less money than a straddle on the same stock and will, therefore, have less dollar risk.

Combination Buying Vs. Straddle Buying

Let's compare the above combination with the purchase of a straddle, using the Apr 50 call and the Apr 50 put as follows:

Buy Apr 50 call at 3¾
Buy Apr 50 put at . . . .<u>3⅜</u>

Total cost 7⅛

The total cost of 7⅛ would also represent the maximum dollar risk, versus the much smaller dollar risk of 3¹/₁₆ for the combination. The 10-point difference between the strike prices of the call and put had the effect of substantially reducing the combination's maximum dollar risk relative to the straddle.

However, while the maximum dollar risk on the combination has been reduced, the area in which some loss would occur has been widened.

Combination Sale Vs. Straddle Sale

Even though the sale of a combination generates a smaller premium for the seller than the sale of a straddle on the same underlying stock, the underlying stock must make a greater move in either direction for his opponent to become profitable.

Chapter 15

PUT MARGINS

What:
Put margins are the minimum deposits required by the regulatory bodies for trading in puts.

Why:
Margin requirements are designed as safeguards for investors so that only financially eligible persons are permitted to engage in different put related transactions with varied risks.

How:
See different margin requirements for (1) long put, (2) long put, long stock, (3) short put, (4) short put, short stock, (5) put spread, (6) straddle, and (7) combination under respective chapters covering such topics.

 1. *Long Put*
  Must be paid for in full.
 2. *Long Put, Long Stock*
  Cash Account: Both the stock and the put must be paid for in full.
  Margin Account: (A) Put must be paid for in full
        (B) Stock on 50% margin.
 3. *Short Put*
  Must be margined as an uncovered call.
 4. *Short Put, Short Stock*
  (A) Put—No margin required
  (B) Stock—50% Margin
 5. *Put Spread*
  Lesser of the following two:
  (A) Excess of short-option exercise price over long-option

exercise price.

(B) Margined as an uncovered short.

6. *Straddle*

(A) *Long Call, Long Put*

Both call and put must be paid for in full.

(B) *Short Call, Short Put*

The uncovered short requirement on the call or the put, whichever is *greater*.

7. *Combination*

30% of stock value *plus* the amount by which either, or both, of the positions are in-the-money. There is no credit allowed if call and/or put are in-the-money.

Minimum Margin Requirements

The New York Stock Exchange and the Option Exchanges have coordinated margin requirements for puts so that member firms can set uniform standards for their customers. It should be emphasized, however, that these are minimum margins (i.e., brokerage firms are prohibited from requiring less from their clients). Typically, many firms require more than the minimum margins used in our illustrations.

Many of the put margins described below are similar to the margin requirements for calls. The illustrations assume an option to be for 100 shares of the underlying stock. For simplicity, the illustrations disregard minimum account equity requirements, which currently mean $2,000 equity in a margin account.

LONG PUT

Under regulatory rules, a long put must be paid for in full, and will not have loan value in a margin account. This is identical to long call requirements.

Illustration

On Nov 28, 1977, Westinghouse (WX) had a July 20 put available at $2^{1}/_{16}$ when the stock traded at 19.

If an investor bought 1 WX July 20 put for $2^{1}/_{16}$, and had no cash or other securities in his cash or margin account, he would be required to deposit $206.25 ($2.0625 × 100) as full payment for the put.

LONG PUT—LONG STOCK

1. Initial Margin Requirement

(1) *Margin Account*

Under Federal Reserve Board rules, the initial margin required for a long put-long stock position in a margin account will be the initial margin requirement (currently 50%) on the stock position. The option must be paid for in full.

(2) *Cash Account*

In a cash account, both the stock and the put must be paid for in full.

2. Maintenance Margin Requirement

The exchange maintenance requirement is 25% of the market value of the stock, with no "mark to the market" provision for the put. "Marking to the market" means that each day your broker will recompute your margin requirement, and if your account requires more money, you must supply it immediately.

It is important to note here that a rapid decline in the price of the stock could require a maintenance call, even though the customer's maximum risk could be the price of the put.

Illustration

On Nov 8, 1977, Avon (AVP) traded at 45 when its July 45 put was 3.

If an investor in a margin account bought 100 shares of AVP for 45, and 1 AVP July 45 put for 3 (i.e., a long put-long stock), the downside risk in this position would be limited to the cost of the put (3) because, during the life of the put, he had the right to "put" (sell) his stock at the exercise price of 45 (at-the-money).

SHORT PUT

A short put must be margined in the same manner as an uncovered call, i.e.,

30% of the value of the underlying stock

plus the amount that the put is in-the-money, or

less the amount that the put is out-of-the-money
with a minimum $250 margin requirement per contract.

Illustration
1. *In-The-Money*
On Nov 28, 1977, Honeywell (HON) traded at 48
when its Aug 50 put (in-the-money) was 4¾:

Strike Price	Put Price	Stock Price
50	4¾	48

In-The-Money
Assuming, with no cash or securities in his margin account, an investor sold a HON Aug 50 put for 4¾, the
margin requirement would be:

30% of stock value (48) $1,440
plus In-the-money amount (50–48) 200

Margin requirement $1,640
less Put premium received (4¾)................ 475

Margin call............................$1,165

Out-Of-The-Money
Using the same Honeywell illustration, HON's Aug 45
put (out-of-the-money) was priced at 2¼ when the stock
was trading at 48:

Strike Price	Put Price	Stock Price
50	2¼	48

(out-of-the-money)
Assuming the same investor sold a HON Aug 45 put
for 2¼, the margin requirement would be:

30% of stock value (48) $1,440
less Out-of-the-money amount (48−45)........... 300

Margin requirement $1,140
less Put premium received (2¼)................. 225

Margin call............................$ 915

158

IV. SHORT PUT—SHORT STOCK

Initial Margin Requirement
Under regulatory rules, the initial margin requirement for a short put-short stock position in a margin account will be 50% (currently) on the short stock position with no margin required on the short put.

Illustration
On Nov 28, 1977, Hughes Tool (HT) traded at 34⅞ when its June 35 put was 3:

Strike Price	Put Price	Stock Price
35	3	34⅞

Assuming an investor with no cash or other securities in his margin account sold short 100 shares of HT for 34⅞, and sold 1 HT June 35 put for 3, his initial margin requirement would be:

```
50% of short-sale stock price (34⅞) .......$1,743.75
less Put premium received (3)...........    300.00

Margin call.........................$1,443.75
```

Maintenance Margin Requirement
Except for low priced stocks (i.e., below $5 per share), the minimum maintenance margin requirement will be 30% of the market value of the short stock position, with no additional margin requirement for the put.

In computing this 30%, the value given to the underlying stock may not be less than the exercise price of the short put, even though the stock price may be below the exercise price of the put.

Here is how to compute the maintenance margin:
Illustration:
Using the above illustration on Hughes Tool, the equity in this investor's account after the $1,443.75 margin call has been met would be $1,743.75.

Should HT rise 10 points from 34⅞ to 44⅞, equity in the account would decrease by the $1,000 loss in the short stock position to $743.75 per the calculation below:

```
Equity in the account .................$1,743.75
less Loss in the short stock position....... 1,000.00

                                       $   743.75
```

At this time, the maintenance margin requirement would be recalculated below:

30% of the stock value (44⅞)	$1,346.25
less Equity in the account	743.75
Maintenance call	$ 602.50

Thus, the investor would be called upon to come up with an additional margin call of $602.50.

On the other hand, should HT decline below the exercise price of 35, the market value of the stock may not be calculated, for margin purposes, at less than the put's exercise price (35). Thus, the maintenance margin in this illustration would not fall below $1,050 (30% of $3,500).

PUT SPREAD MARGINS

General Spread Margin Rules

A put spread is the simultaneous purchase and sale of puts of different series within the same class. Spreads can be executed only in margin accounts.

A position is considered a spread for margin purposes
(1) If both the long and short positions are of the same class, and
(2) If the long option expires no earlier than the short option.

In addition to the $2,000 minimum initial margin (which applies to spreads), the long option must be paid for in full.

Margins For Put Spreads

The margin required on a put spread position is the *lesser* of the following:
(A) The amount by which the exercise price of the short option is above the exercise price of the long option.
(B) The amount that would be required to margin the short position if it were an uncovered short, i.e.,
  30% of the stock price
  plus the amount the short put is in-the-money, or
  minus the amount the short put is out-of-the-money,
      with a minimum $250 per contract.

Illustrations

1. *In-The-Money*

On Nov 28, 1977, Honeywell (HON) had the following Aug 45 and Aug 50 puts when the stock traded at 48:

Strike Price	Put Price	Stock Price
45	2¼	48
50	4¾	48

Assuming an investor sold 1 Aug 50 put for 4¾ and bought 1 Aug 45 put for 2¼, the required margin would be:

(1) Under Rule (A) above:

Difference in exercise prices (50−45) $500

less the premium received................... 475

Margin call ....$ 25

(2) under Rule (B) above:

30% of the stock price (48) $1,440

plus In-the-money amount of short option 200

Margin required $1,640

less Premium received.......................... 475

Margin call...............................$1,165

Since the required margin is the *lesser* of the above, the $25 margin under Rule (A) would be required of this investor in addition to the $475 premium received.

If, however, the investor had no cash or other securities in the account, the margin call would be for $1,525 per the calculation below:

Minimum margin requirement $2,000

less the premium received 475

$1,525

2. *Out-Of-The-Money*

On Nov 18, 1977, Revlon (REV) had the following Mar 35 and 40 puts when the stock traded at 43:

Strike Price	Put Price	Stock Price
35	7/16	43
40	1½	43

Assuming an investor sold 1 Mar 40 put for 1½ and 1 Mar 35 put for ⁷/₁₆, the required margin would be:

(1) Under Rule (A) above:

Difference in exercise prices (40−35) $500
less the premium received................... 150

Margin call $350

(2) Under Rule (B) above:

30% of the stock price (43) $1,290
less out-of-the-money amount
of short option   800

Margin required........................ 490
less premium received 150

Margin call $340

Since the required margin is the *lesser* of the above, the $340 margin under Rule (B) would be required in addition to the $150 premium received.

If, however, the investor had no cash or other securities in the account, the margin call would be $1,850 per calculation below:

Minimum margin requirement...............$2,000
less the premium received 150

$1,850

STRADDLE MARGINS

A straddle is the purchase or sale of both a call and a put on the same underlying stock, with the same strike price and the same expiration date.

Long Call—Long Put

If a straddle involves a long call and a long put, both the call and the put, under regulatory rules, must be paid for in full and neither will have loan value in a margin account.

Illustration

On Nov 29, 1977, IBM had the following Apr 260 call and put when the stock traded at 262¾:

	Strike Price	Option Price
Call	260	12¼
Put	260	7¾

If an investor, who had no cash or other securities in his cash or margin account, bought 1 IBM Apr 260 call for 12¼ and 1 IBM Apr 260 put for 7¾, he would be required to deposit $2,000 per the calculation below as full payment for the call and the put.

Buy Apr 260 call (12¼ × 100 shares) $1,225
Buy Apr 260 put (7¾ × 100 shares) 775

Total premiums required $2,000

Short Call—Short Put

If a straddle involves a short call and a short put, the required margin will be the uncovered short requirement on the call or the put, whichever is *greater*.

Illustration:

On Nov 28, 1977, Eastman Kodak (EK) had the following July 50 call and put when EK traded at 53:

	Strike Price	Option Price	Stock Price
Call	50	6½	53
Put	50	2½	53

If an investor who had no cash or securities in his margin account sold 1 EK July 50 call for 6½ and 1 EK July 50 put for 2½ when the stock traded at 53, the required margin would be the *greater* of the following two computations:

(1) Call Computation

30% of stock price (53) $1,590
plus Call *in-the-money* amount (53–50)....... 300

Margin requirement $1,890
less Premium received (6½ + 2½) 900

Margin call ....$ 990

(2) Put Computation
30% of stock value (53) $1,590
less put *out-of-the-money* amount
(53−50) 300

Margin requirement $1,290
less premium received (6½ + 2½) 900

$ 390

The *greater* of the call computation ($990) and of the put computation ($390) is $990—the margin call which must be issued.

COMBINATION MARGINS

Short Call, Short Put with Different Exercise Prices
A combination is either the purchase, or the sale, of both puts and calls (on the same underlying stock) that have different strike prices and the same, or different expiration months.

The required margin for a combination is
30% of the market value of the underlying stock
plus the amount by which either, or
both, of the positions are in-the-money.
There is no credit allowed if the call and/or the put are out-of-the-money.

Illustration:
On Nov 8, 1977, Avon (AVP) had the following Apr 40 call and Apr 50 put when AVP traded at 45:

	Strike Price	Option Price	Stock Price
Call	40	4	45
	(in-the-money)		
Put	50		
	(in-the-money)	5	45

If an investor sold two Apr 40 calls and two Apr 50 puts, the required margin would be:

30% of the stock price (2 × 45)	$2,700
plus Put *in-the-money* amount (2 × 5)	1,000
plus Call *in-the-money* amount (2 × 5)	1,000

| Margin requirement .... | $4,700 |
| *less* Premiums received (2 × 9).................... | 1,800 |

| Margin call .... | $2,900 |

The rationale behind the margin requirement reflecting both the in-the-money amount and the out-of-the-money amount is that, if both sides were to be exercised, there would be a 10-point risk in each of the two options. This risk, therefore, must be built into the margin requirement.

GLOSSARY OF OPTION TERMS

Accumulation:
> The process by which an excess supply of stock is absorbed by an expanding demand that over time has a favorable effect on the price of the stock.

Arbitrage:
> Option trading to take advantage of a temporary price discrepancy between options, or between the option and the underlying stock.

Asked: The price at which someone demands for selling a certain option.

At-the-money:
> An option is said to be "at the money" when its strike price (or exercise price) is the same as the price of the underlying security.

Bank Guarantee Letter:
> Letter issued by an exchange approved bank certifying that the writer of a put has cash on deposit at that bank to cover the purchase of the underlying stock, should the option be exercised or, in the case of a call, that the writer has deposited the underlying stock with the bank. The bank will deliver the stock upon exercise.

Bear Market:
> A long period, often a year or more, in which the general trend of securities prices is down.

Bear Spread:
> This strategy involves the simultaneous purchase of one type of option, put or call, and the sale of another of the same type—both on the same stock. The purchased option must have a higher strike price than the sold option. Both should have identical expiration dates. This strategy is based on an investor's expectation of a decline in the stock price.

Bearish:

The approach of an investor who believes a stock or stocks will decline.

Beta:

A measure of the stock's sensitivity to the movement of the general market in recent years.

Bid:

The price someone is willing to pay for a particular option.

Bull Market:

A long period, usually a year or more, in which the general trend of securities prices is up.

Bull Spread:

This strategy involves the simultaneous purchase of one type of option, put or call, and the sale of another of the same type—both on the same stock. The purchased option must have a lower strike price than the sold option; both should have identical expiration dates.

Bullish:

The approach of an investor who believes a stock or stocks will advance.

Buyer:

The person who purchases an option.

Buying A Spread:

To put on a spread at a debit; when an investor pays out more than is received. It occurs when an investor buys the more expensive of two options, and sells the less expensive.

Buying A Straddle:

To purchase a put and a call covering the same underlying security, and having the same exercise price and expiration date.

Calendar Spread:

Also known as a time spread or horizontal spread. It involves simultaneous purchase and sale of options on the same underlying stock, which have the same strike price but different expiration dates.

Call:

A contract to buy 100 shares of a specified stock at a specific price (the exercise or strike price) at any time within a given period of time.

Called:

Another term for exercised. The writer of a call must deliver the indicated underlying security when the option is exercised or called.

Classes Of Options:
Options of the same type (call or put) covering the same underlying security.

Close-to-The-Money:
The strike price of the option is close to the current price of the underlying stock. Time value, as a factor in determining the premium, is at its maximum.

Closing Sale:
A transaction in which an investor wishes to liquidate an option position as an option holder by selling an option having the same terms as the option originally purchased.

Combinations:
Any strategy involving the purchase or sale of both puts and calls.

Consolidation:
A pause in a trend, with the expectation that the trend will be resumed in the same direction.

Correction:
A price decline or pull back, or a price reaction.

Cover:
To purchase stock, or an option on it, in order to fulfill a naked commitment.

Covered Call Writer:
A writer of a call option who owns the underlying stock (long the stock) upon which the option is written.

Covered Put Writer:
The writer of a put option who owns another put on the same underlying stock—with the same or higher exercise price.

Cycle:
The months in which options expire. Currently there are two cycles on the CBOE: The January, April, July, October and the February, May, August, November cycles.

Demand:
The degree of investor interest in purchasing a stock.

Diagonal Spread:
A combination of time and price spreads. It involves the simultaneous purchase and sale of options of the same class

which have different exercise prices and different expiration dates.

Downmove:

The action of a stock or option from a higher to a lower price level.

Downside:

Toward a downward move.

Exercise:

To place into effect the option rights held by an option buyer. To request the writer to deliver stock at the stated price (call), or to pay the stated price for stock delivered to him (put).

Exercise Notice:

Written statement on an option holder's intention to exercise the option.

Exercise Price (strike price):

The price per share at which the option buyer may buy, in the case of a call, or sell, in the case of a put, 100 shares of the underlying stock.

Expiration Date:

Sometimes called expiration time. The date on which the put or call option contract expires. Expiration dates are standardized, and are always three months apart. No more than three expiration dates are traded on a particular option at a particular time.

Expiration Month:

The months in which options expire.

Fundamental:

Information about a company's profitability, balance sheet strength, management and industry outlook.

Good-Until-Canceled Orders:

They are limit orders which are valid for the life of the designated option contract, until they are canceled.

Hedge:

A means of protecting against financial loss, usually by offsetting a long (buy) position in one stock or option with a short (sell) position in a related stock or option.

Horizontal Spread:

See time spread.

In-The-Money:

An option is said to be in-the-money when it has intrinsic

value. A call option is in-the-money if the underlying security's price is greater than the option's exercise price. A put option is in-the-money if the underlying security's price is lower than the option's exercise price.

Initial Margin:
The minimum margin required when an option transaction is initiated. Long calls and long puts must be paid in full. CBOE regulations require a $2,000 initial equity in a margin account when a new transaction is effected. Thereafter, maintenance requirements come into consideration.

Intermediate Term:
Three to six months.

Intrinsic Value:
The difference between the current stock price and the striking price of the option. A call option is said to have intrinsic value when the stock price is greater than the exercise price. A put option is said to have intrinsic value when the stock price falls below the exercise price.

Leverage:
To attain a large profit potential per investment dollar.

Limit Order:
Orders to buy or sell at a specified price or better.

Limited Risk:
The fact that option buyers can never lose more than the initial cost of the option.

Long Option:
An option that has been purchased.

Long Term:
More than six months.

Maintenance Margin:
The minimum equity a margin account must maintain.

Margin:
The amount the investor must deposit with the broker in order to buy or sell stocks. Naked call writers must deliver to their brokers shares worth at least 30% of the value of the securities if the call is exercised. Many brokers require a higher amount.

"Mark To The Market":
It means that each day your broker will recompute your margin requirement, and if your account requires more money you must supply it immediately.

Married Put:

Put and stock acquired on the same day. The stock must be identified as intended to be used in connection with the exercise of the put. The holding period of the stock is figured in the normal manner, unaffected by the existence of the put.

Medium:

See Intermediate terms.

Momentum:

A sustained movement by a stock or the market, either up or down.

Money Spread:

See Price Spread.

Naked Call Writers:

The writer of a call option. In the case of a call, an option in which the writer does not own the underlying security upon which the option is written. See Uncovered Call Writer and Uncovered Put Writer.

Near Term:

Usually three to five weeks.

Neutral Approach:

The strategy an investor uses when it is thought the stock's value will not move appreciably over the near term.

Odd Lot:

A trade of under 100 shares.

On-The-Money:

The exercise price of the option is equal to the market price of the underlying stock. Also known as at-the-money.

Opening Purchase:

A transaction in which an investor intends to become the holder of an option.

Opening Sale:

A transaction in which an investor intends to become a writer (seller) of an option.

Option:

A business contract that allows the buyer to buy or sell stock (in 100-share units) at a certain price (known as the Exercise Price or Strike Price) over a certain period, regardless of how high or low the price of the stock (known as the underlying security) moves during that time.

Out-Of-the-Money:
The exercise price of the call is higher than the market price of the underlying stock, or the exercise price of the put is lower than the current stock price.

Over-The-Counter Options (OTC):
Non-listed put and call options whose expiration dates and exercise prices are not standardized. OTC options are not cleared or guaranteed by the OCC.

Parity:
This refers to the situation in which the market price of the stock equals the exercise (strike) price of the option, plus the option premium (price).

Premium:
The price that the buyer pays the seller (writer) for the right (option) to sell stock to him at a later date and at a specific price (puts), or buy stock from him (calls).

Price Spread:
A spread involving the purchase and sale of options of the same class having common expiration dates, but different exercise prices. Also known as money spread or vertical spread.

Put (or Put Option):
The right to sell to the writer the stated number of shares (typically 100) of the underlying security within a stated period of time at the stated exercise price. Puts are usually acquired when the buyer expects a stock to decline during the life of the option.

Ratio Spread:
A spread strategy in which the number of contracts sold differs from the number purchased. The contracts are the same type (puts or calls), and are identical except for strike price. Also known as variable spread.

Reaction:
Price movement in the opposite direction to a stock's overall trend, which corrects an overbought or oversold condition.

Resistance:
A price level at which potential sellers may overcome demand and temporarily stop or reverse an advance.

Risk/Reward Ratio:
A potential loss relative to a potential gain in a proposed strategy, expressed as a ratio.

172

Secondary Market:

A marketplace for the disposal (selling or buying) of previously bought or sold options through closing transactions.

Sell A Spread:

When an investor receives more than is paid by selling the more expensive of the two options in a spread and buying the less expensive. Known as "putting the spread on at a credit."

Series of Options:

Options of the same class having the same exercise price and expiration month.

Short Position:

To write an option, or sell underlying stock without actually owning the stock at the time of the transaction.

Short Option:

An option that has been sold.

Short Put:

Selling a put option.

Spread:

The simultaneous purchase and sale of options on the same underlying stock. These may have the same strike price with different expiration months, or may have different prices with the same or different expirations. The spread itself is the amount spent for the buy premiums and that gained on the sell premiums.

Stop Point:

The stock price which triggers investor action, should the shares of the stock reach that price.

Straddle:

Purchase or sale of an equal number of puts and calls on the same underlying stock, with identical exercise prices and expiration dates.

Strike Price:

See Exercise Price.

Support:

A price level at which potential buyers, expecting an upturn
• on the basis of a stock's historical performance, become active enough to temporarily stop or reverse a decline.

Time Spread:

Spreads between options with the same exercise price, but

different expiration dates. Also known as Calendar or Horizontal Spread.

Time Value:
That part of an option premium that reflects the remaining life of the option. The more time that remains before the expiration date, the higher the premium, because of more time available for the value of the underlying security to change.

Uncovered Call Writer:
A call writer is considered to be uncovered (naked) when that writer does not own the underlying security upon which the option is written or a long call of the same class, with an equal or lesser exercise price. See "Naked Option".

Uncovered Put Writer:
A put writer is considered to be uncovered (naked) when that writer does not hold a long put of the same class, with an equal or higher exercise price.

Underlying Security:
A security underlying an option contract against which a call or put option is traded.

Upmove:
The action of a stock or option from a lower to a higher price level.

Upside:
Toward an upward move.

Variable Hedging:
Writing more than one option for every 100 shares of the underlying security owned by the writer.

Variable Spread:
Spreads in which the number of contracts purchased are different from the number of contracts sold.

Vertical Spread:
The simultaneous purchase and sale of options on the same underlying stock, which have the same expiration date, but different strike prices. Also known as price or money spread.

Writer of Option:
An investor who grants option privileges to the buyer in exchange for the premium.

Yield:
The return which the investor can expect on his investment.

174

PUT OPTIONS QUESTIONNAIRE

On What To Focus

Just as we did with my previous book, HOW TO MAKE MONEY IN LISTED OPTIONS, the PUT OPTIONS QUESTIONNAIRE is designed to help the reader know what to focus on in the course of studying the subjects covered in this book.

Question-and-Answer Method

To achieve the best results, it is suggested that the focusing be done by the reader asking himself the following series of salient questions and seeking answers in the course of reading the book.

Considerable Skill

This method of reading with a "focus" appears particularly appropriate for a subject matter such as put options that requires considerable skill and exercises to reach deeper layers of put buying, writing, straddling, and spreading techniques, and to uncover their ever-widening interfacing applications.

In Chapter Sequence

To facilitate our readers in learning by asking-and-answering questions, we arrange the Questionnaire in chapter order.

I. ON PUTS BASICS

1. What is a listed put option?
2. Why do listed puts result in greater investment flexibility?
3. Why do listed puts enable investors to trade for profit in "down" markets as in "up" markets?
4. What is the importance of a listed market for puts?
5. Why is a put the mirror image of a call?

6. What are the similarities between a put and a call?
7. What are the major differences between a put and a call?
8. What is an in-the-money put?
9. What is an out-of-the-money put?
10. What is the relationship between put premium and stock price?
11. What are the major factors determining put premiums?
12. What is the volatility of a stock? How do you measure it?
13. Why is volatility important to put buying or selling?

II. ON FOCUSING ON SIMPLE STRATEGIES

14. What are the basic strategies using puts?
15. What are the two basic strategies from the put buyer's viewpoint?
16. What are the two basic strategies from the put seller's viewpoint?
17. What are the two principal advantages a put buyer has over a short seller in the underlying stock?
18. What is the principal reason for combining a put purchase with buying the underlying stock?
19. Why should one sell a put?
20. What is the principal reason for combining a put sale with selling short the underlying stock?

III. ON PUT BUYING: WHY & HOW

21. How does an investor profit from an anticipated decline in the price of a certain stock?
22. Why is put buying analogous to buying "insurance"?
23. Why is put buying a particularly useful protection in connection with purchase of volatile stocks?
24. What's the maximum risk in put buying?
25. What are the similarities between a put buyer and a call buyer?
26. What are the differences between a put buyer and a call buyer?
27. What's the meaning of covered put buying?
28. What's the meaning of uncovered put buying?

IV. ON LONG PUT

29. What is a "long put"?
30. What are the principal uses of buying puts as a trading vehicle?
31. What would happen to a put buyer if the stock price at expiration is (1) below the strike price, or (2) above the strike price?
32. How do you dispose of a profitable "long put" position?
33. How do you "exercise" a "long put" position?
34. What is the alternate way to benefit from a profitable "long put" position other than "exercising" it?
35. Where is the "resale" market for puts?
36. What is the third possible approach to exercise or resale?
37. Why is put purchase an alternative to short sale in the underlying stock?
38. What are the two main advantages of put purchase over short sale?
39. Does stop-loss order have any advantages? What are its disadvantages?
40. Compare the leverage factor in put buying with that in short sale.
41. What's the meaning of "depreciation factor"? How to calculate it?
42. Compare the risk factor in put buying with that in short sale.
43. Compare put buying with short sale regarding margin calls, timing flexibility, taxes and cash dividend liability.

V. ON LONG PUT, LONG STOCK

44. What's the purpose of simultaneously owning a common stock and a put on the same stock?
45. How can a long put position allow an investor to pursue long-term investment objectives?
46. Why does only put buying provide the complete hedge to a long stock position?
47. What are the two principal applications for a combined long stock-long put strategy?
48. How do you protect unrealized profit in a stock position

177

which an investor does not want to relinquish?

49. How do you freeze a capital gain or loss in stock in a current year and defer the tax consequences to the succeeding year?
50. How do you establish a stock position while establishing a minimum price for its possible liquidation?
51. What's the meaning of "married put"?
52. Compare long put plus long stock on the one hand with long put plus long call on the other.

VI. ON PUT SELLING: WHY & HOW

53. What kind of underlying stock does one look for when selling a put?
54. What are the two types of put selling?
55. What is an uncovered put?
56. Why does naked put selling place the seller in the same economic position as a "conservative" covered call writer?
57. Compare the risk-reward factors of a covered call writer with those of an uncovered put writer.
58. What is the meaning of "covered" put selling?
59. Is "covered" put selling completely "covered"?
60. What are the two principal purposes of put selling?
61. How does a put seller choose the exercise price (1) if he is bullish on the underlying stock, or (2) if he is bearish?
62. What is the obligation of a put seller?
63. What does the put seller do when he receives an exercise notice?
64. What's the meaning of a "closing purchase transaction"?

VII. ON SHORT PUT

65. What is a "short put"?
66. Why does a put seller need ample cash reserve?
67. Why is "naked" put selling more conservative than its name indicates?
68. What are the two principal ways for a put seller to realize his premium income?
69. How can an investor buy stock at a price below the market price?

70. What is the inherent risk for a put seller with a related stock position?
71. What are the means of defense available to put sellers to minimize their exposure?

VIII. ON SHORT PUT, SHORT STOCK

72. What is "covered" put selling?
73. Why is "covered" put selling only partially "covered"?
74. Why is "short put, short stock" a bear put strategy?

IX. ON SHORT PUT, LONG STOCK

75. When does an investor sell a put against a long stock position?
76. How does leverage work both ways when an investor sells a put with a position in the related stock?

X. ON PUT SPREADING: WHY & HOW

77. What is put spreading?
78. Does the basic concept of call spreading apply to put spreading?
79. Explain why a spread is essentially the dollar difference between the buy and sell premiums?
80. What is the meaning of "debit" and "credit"?
81. What is the meaning of "even" spread?
82. Why does spreading enable an investor to trade in more volatile stocks without paying high premiums?
83. Why has the appeal of option spreading been enhanced by margin rules?
84. Why is the cost of spreading high?
85. What is the simple formula for calculating potential spread profit?
86. What is the simple formula for calculating potential spread risk?
87. How do you calculate spread breakeven point?
88. In a bear put price spread, why does the spreader buy a

higher strike-price put and sell a lower strike-price put?

89. What is the basic formula for structuring a bear put time spread?

90. How do you roll down a bear put price spread when it becomes profitable?

XI. PUT TIME SPREADS

91. What is put time spreading?

92. How do you structure (1) a bull put time spread, and (2) a bear put time spread?

93. What are the key factors determining the potential profitability in a put time spread?

94. What are the things to watch for in initiating a put time spread?

95. When does a put time spreader use (1) an in-the-money put? (2) an out-of-the-money put? (3) an at-the-money put?

XII. PUT PRICE SPREADS

96. What is a put price spread?

97. Why is a price spread also called a vertical spread?

98. How do you construct a put price spread?

99. In a bullish put price spread, why does the spreader sell a higher strike-price put and buy a lower strike-price put?

100. Why is a spread essentially a risk-reducing device?

XIII. ON STRADDLES

101. How do listed puts facilitate trading in straddles?

102. What is the option strategy enabling investors to make money without knowing market direction?

103. When does one buy a straddle? And sell a straddle?

104. Why do straddles provide a means of making money both for the buyer and for the seller?

105. What is a long straddle?

106. Why does a straddle buyer need a substantial move (in either direction) in the underlying stock?

107. How do you calculate the upper and lower profit levels for a straddle buyer?
108. Why is volatility in the underlying stock the key to successful straddle buying?
109. How do you choose the expiration month in straddle buying?
111. What kind of market action does a straddle seller anticipate in the underlying stock?
112. What are the two principal motivations for selling a straddle?
113. How do you calculate the profit parameters for a straddle seller?
114. When does the maximum profit for a straddle seller occur?
115. How do you reduce risk in selling a straddle through use of varied strike prices for the call and the put?
116. Why does "whipshaw" pose a major risk for a straddle seller?
117. Why does one use an out-of-the-money option in structuring a bullish straddle?
118. Why does one use an in-the-money option in structuring a bearish straddle?

XIV. ON COMBINATIONS

119. What is a combination?
120. Should combination buyers and sellers look for the same characteristics in selecting a stock?
121. What is the purpose of combination buying?
122. What is the purpose of combination selling?
123. What is the importance of volatility to combination buying or selling?
124. How do you structure a combination on the same expiration month?
125. How do you calculate the profit parameters for a combination buyer or seller?
126. Compare a combination with a straddle.
127. How do you incorporate a bullish or bearish bias into combination buying?
128. Why does one use a call closer to being in-the-money when structuring a bullish combination-buying position?

129. Why does one use a put closer to being in-the-money when structuring a bearish combination-buying position?
130. What are the different expectations for a combination buyer with or without holding a position in the underlying stock?
131. What is the step-by-step procedure for combination buying?
132. What is the meaning of "lifting a leg" for a combination buyer?
133. What is the maximum risk for a combination buyer?
134. Why does a bullish combination seller use a stable stock?
135. What is covered combination selling?
136. What is uncovered combination selling?
137. What is the motivation for a covered combination seller?
138. What is the motivation for an uncovered combination seller?
139. Why does a bullish combination seller use a put closer to being in-the-money?
140. Why does a bearish combination seller use a call closer to being in-the-money?

XV. ON PUT MARGINS

141. What is the margin requirement for a long put?
142. What is the margin requirement for a long put, long stock?
143. What is the margin requirement for a short put?
144. What is the margin requirement for a short put, short stock?
145. What is the margin requirement for a put spread?
146. What is the margin requirement for a straddle?
147. What is the margin requirement for a combination?